HIGH STAKES: writing

Candace S. Baker

THOMSON

PETERSON'S

Australia • Canada • Mexico • Singapore • Spain • United Kingdom • United States

About The Thomson Corporation and Peterson's

With revenues of US$7.2 billion, The Thomson Corporation (www.thomson.com) is a leading global provider of integrated information solutions for business, education, and professional customers. Its Learning businesses and brands (www.thomsonlearning.com) serve the needs of individuals, learning institutions, and corporations with products and services for both traditional and distributed learning.

Peterson's, part of The Thomson Corporation, is one of the nation's most respected providers of lifelong learning online resources, software, reference guides, and books. The Education Supersite℠ at www.petersons.com—the Internet's most heavily traveled education resource—has searchable databases and interactive tools for contacting U.S.-accredited institutions and programs. In addition, Peterson's serves more than 105 million education consumers annually.

For more information, contact Peterson's, 2000 Lenox Drive, Lawrenceville, NJ 08648; 800-338-3282; or find us on the World Wide Web at www.petersons.com/about.

ISBN 0-7689-1073-0

Printed in the United States of America

10 9 8 7 6 5 4 3 2 1   05 04 03

CONTENTS

CONTENTS

BEFORE YOU GET STARTED

Directions: Choose from **(A)**, **(B)**, **(C)**, or **(D)** the words that make the completed sentence most accurate.

High Stakes tests are

(A) performed by supermarkets to ensure the highest quality beef for their customers.

(B) administered by vampire slayers to ensure the demise of their enemies.

(C) very tall poles.

(D) taken by students to determine whether they are ready to graduate from high school.

We're going to take a wild guess that you chose **(D)** as the correct answer.

All kidding aside, we refer to the exit-level proficiency exams as **"high stakes"** tests because your high school diploma is *at stake*. Your diploma is probably the most valuable piece of paper you'll ever have in your hands. Without it, you may be limited in the kind of work you can do as an adult, and you also won't earn as much money as people who have diplomas. So, unless you're the next Britney Spears or one of those lucky people who wins the million-dollar lottery, these tests *are* high stakes for you.

We're not going to lie to you. Most of the test questions on your exit-level exams will not be as easy to answer as the question above. We're sure you already know that. But we'd bet that you *don't* know what kind of questions will pop up on these exams. And this is one case where what you don't know *can* hurt you.

But not to worry. We have diligently studied the standards for **math, reading, writing,** and **science** skills set by the state educational professionals, as well as the test questions that appear on these exams. We're not only going to tell you what you will be tested *on* but also *how* you will be tested. So, whether your state is going to use multiple-choice questions, essays, or open-ended response, if you've got a *High Stakes* skill book in your hands, we've got you covered.

So that's the good news . . .

But here's even better news! Unlike the SAT, which tests "critical thinking," the state proficiency exams test only what you've learned in school. It's actually pretty hard to study for something as vague as *critical thinking,* which is why you'll find that most SAT test-prep books are full of tricks on how to squeeze out a couple of hundred more points on the test. But the exit-level proficiency exams test **real subject knowledge**. That's not vague, that's simple! And if you've bought this book, we're going to assume you're prepared for some review. So, the bottom line is that if you study the material we give you in this book (which is not that big, right?), you can do more than just pass these exams—you can score high!

Let's Get Organized

The organization of this book is really straightforward. The book is divided into three parts:

Part I provides a short guide to the state exit-level exams and a chapter on strategies and tips to help you plan your study and alleviate test anxiety.

Part II reviews all the topics that will be covered on your state exam.

Part III contains lots of practice questions to help you get comfortable answering the test questions on high stakes exams. We also give you answers and explanations to make sure you understand everything.

Now that you know you can rely on us to help you succeed, we hope we've reduced your stress level. So . . . sit down, take a deep breath, and . . . *relax.* We're going to take you step-by-step through everything you need to know for test day.

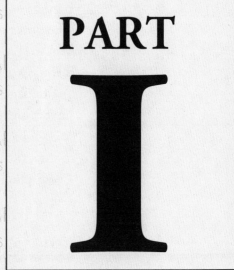

PART I

INTRODUCTION

CHAPTER 1

ALPHABET CITY

Have you checked out the shaded bands on the top of the pages in this book? You'll see some pretty odd combinations of letters, such as TAAS, BST, FCAT, OGT, CAHSEE, and MEAP.

MEAP? What the heck is that? Sounds like Martian for salad or something.

More likely you've recognized some of the letters because they are *acronyms,* which means they are letters that stand for the name of your state exam. MEAP, by the way, stands for Michigan Educational Assessment Program. You have to admit that *Meap* rolls off the tongue a bit more easily.

In this chapter, we list all sixteen states that require exams for graduating high school. Each of the high-stakes states (can you say that 5 times fast?) sets its own rules for the exams, and you'll find some students may appear to have it easier than others. North Carolina tests its students in reading and math only, and the question types are multiple choice only. Students in Minnesota, however, are tested in reading, math, *and* writing, and the question types include multiple choice, short answer, *and* essays! But don't worry, beginning in 2005, students in North Carolina will be tested in reading, math, science, social studies, English, *and* grammar. Perhaps that's why the official state beverage of North Carolina is milk . . . those students will need their strength!

The point is that you should look carefully at the rules for your own state. For example, if you're one of those lucky North Carolinians taking the test in 2003 or 2004, you can skip any practice question that is not multiple choice. As we said earlier, it's our job to make sure we cover all the bases for everyone, but you only have to study what you're actually being tested on.

You may have to take other subject tests in high school, which are not required for graduation. Some tests are for advanced diplomas (such as the Regents Math B). Other tests are actually testing your teachers and your school system. We're here to help you graduate, and we focus only on the tests where the stakes are high for *you*.

> **Log on to www.petersons.com/highstakes for your Graduation Checklist, which will highlight information you need to have on your state's scoring, test dates, required topics of study, and more!**

The following list of states is in alphabetical order.

Alabama

Exit-Level Exam: Alabama High School Graduation Exam (**AHSGE**)

State Education Department Website: www.alsde.edu

Students take the AHSGE in eleventh grade. Beginning with the graduating class of 2003, students must pass all subject-area tests in order to graduate. Students have six opportunities to take these exams.

Test	# Questions	Time	Question Type
Reading	84	approx. 3 hrs.	multiple choice
Language	100	approx. 3 hrs.	multiple choice
Science	100	approx. 3 hrs.	multiple choice
Math	100	approx. 3 hrs.	multiple choice
Social Studies	100	approx. 3 hrs.	multiple choice

California

Exit-Level Exam: California High School Exit Exam (**CAHSEE**)

State Education Department Website: www.cde.ca.gov

Students take the CAHSEE in tenth grade. As of the 2003–04 school year, students are required to pass both parts of the CAHSEE. Students have multiple opportunities to retake one or both portions of the exam.

Test	# Questions	Time	Question Type
English-Language	82	untimed	multiple choice
English-Language	2	untimed	short essays (includes written response to text and prompt)
Math	80	untimed	multiple choice

Florida

Exit-Level Exam: Florida Comprehensive Assessment Test (**FCAT**)

State Education Department Website: www.firn.edu/doe/sas/fcat

Students take the FCAT in tenth grade and must pass the reading and math parts of the exam in order to graduate. Students have multiple opportunities to retake the exams.

Test	# Questions	Time	Question Type
Reading	105	untimed	multiple choice
Math	100	untimed	multiple choice

Georgia

Exit-Level Exam: Georgia High School Graduation Tests (**GHSGT**)

State Education Department Website: www.doe.k12.ga.us/sla/ret/ghsgt.asp

Students take the GHSGT in eleventh grade and must pass each of the 5 tests in order to graduate. Students have five opportunities to take each of the tests before the end of twelfth grade.

Test	# Questions	Time	Question Type
English/ Language Arts	50	3 hrs. max	multiple choice
Math	60	3 hrs. max.	multiple choice
Social Studies	80	3 hrs. max.	multiple choice
Science	70	3 hrs. max.	multiple choice
Writing	1	90 mins.	essay

Louisiana

Exit-Level Exam: Graduation Exit Examination for the 21st Century (**GEE 21**)

State Education Department Website: www.doe.state.la.us

Students take the GEE 21 in the tenth grade (English language arts *and* mathematics) and must pass them both to graduate. Students also take the GEE 21 in the eleventh grade (science *or* social studies) and must pass one of these to graduate. Students have multiple opportunities to retake each portion of the exam.

Test	# Questions	Time	Question Type
English / Language Arts	61	untimed	multiple choice and essay

Math	60	untimed	multiple choice and short answer
Science	44	untimed	multiple choice and short answer
Social Studies	64	untimed	multiple choice and short answer

Massachusetts

Exit-Level Exam: Massachusetts Comprehensive Assessment System (**MCAS**)

State Education Department Website: www.doe.mass.edu/mcas

Students take the MCAS in the tenth grade and must pass the English Language Arts and Math portions of the exam in order to graduate. Students have multiple opportunities to retake both portions of the test.

Test	# Questions	Time	Question Type
Math	51	untimed	multiple choice, short answer, and open response
English/ Language Arts	55	untimed	multiple choice and writing prompt

Michigan

Exit-Level Exam: Michigan Educational Assessment Program High School Tests (MEAP HST)

State Education Department Website: www.meritaward.state.mi.us/mma/ meap.htm

Students take the MEAP HST in eleventh grade and must pass all parts of the exam in order to graduate. Students have the opportunity to retake portions of the exam in the twelfth grade.

Test	# Questions	Time	Question Type
Math	43	100 min.	multiple choice and open response
Reading*	29	80 min.	multiple choice and open response
Science	50	90 min.	multiple choice and open response
Social Studies	42	80 min.	multiple choice and open response
Writing*	2	120 min.	open response

*As of the 2003–04 school year, Reading and Writing will be combined into an English Language Arts test along with a Listening test.

Minnesota

Exit-Level Exam: Basic Skills Test (**BST**)

State Education Department Website: http://cflapp.state.mn.us/CLASS/stds/assessments/bst/index.jsp

Students take the math and reading portions of the BST in eighth grade and the writing portion in tenth grade and must pass all portions of the exam in order to graduate. Students have multiple opportunities to retake each section of the exam.

Test	# Questions	Time	Question Type
Reading	40	120–150 min.	multiple choice and short answer
Writing	several	90–120 min.	short essays
Math	68	120–150 min.	multiple choice and short answer

New Jersey

Exit-Level Exam: High School Proficiency Assessment (**HSPA**)

State Education Department Website: www.state.nj.us/education

Students take the HSPA in eleventh grade and must pass both sections in order to graduate. In 2004–05, a social studies assessment will be phased in, and in March 2005, science will be added. Students have two additional opportunities to retake each portion of the exam in their senior year.

Test	# Questions	Time	Question Type
Language Arts/ Literacy	55	4 hrs.	multiple choice and open ended
Mathematics	48	2 hrs.	multiple choice and open ended

New York

Exit-Level Exam: Regents Exams

State Education Department Website: www.emsc.nysed.gov/deputy/Documents/ alternassess.htm

Students take the Regents in tenth and eleventh grades and must pass the five Regents Examinations listed below to graduate. In general, students in the tenth grade are tested in science, math, and global history and geography. Students in the eleventh grade are tested in English language arts, and U.S. history and government. Students who fail portions of the exam twice are required to pass a component test for that portion in order to graduate.

Test	# Questions	Time	Question Type
English	29	3 hrs.	multiple choice and essay
Math	35	3 hrs.	multiple choice and open ended

Global History and Geography	60–62	3 hrs.	multiple choice and open ended
U.S. History and Government	60–62	3 hrs.	multiple choice and open ended
Science	62–94	3 hrs.	multiple choice and open ended

North Carolina

Exit-Level Exam: North Carolina Competency Tests (**NCCT**)

State Education Department Website: www.ncpublicschools.org/accountability/testing/policies/

Students take the NCCT in eighth grade. Students who do not pass may retake portions of the test three times each year in grades 9–11 and four times in twelfth grade in order to graduate. Passing scores in both portions of the exam are needed in order to graduate.

Test	# Questions	Time	Question Type
Reading	156	1 hr. 40 mins.	multiple choice
Math	165	1 hr. 40 mins.	multiple choice

Ohio

Exit-Level Exam: Ninth Grade Proficiency Tests and Ohio Graduation Tests (**OGT**)

State Education Department Website: www.ode.state.oh.us

Students take the Ninth Grade Proficiency Tests and must pass all of the portions to graduate. Beginning in the 2003–04 school year, students will take the exams (to be renamed OGT) in the tenth grade and are also required to pass all portions of the exam to graduate. Students have multiple opportunities to retake portions of both the Ninth Grade Proficiency Tests and the OGT.

Test	# Questions	Time	Question Type
Writing	2	2.5 hrs.	essay
Reading	49	2.5 hrs.	multiple choice and open response
Math	50	2.5 hrs.	multiple choice and open response
Science	50	2.5 hrs.	multiple choice and open response
Citizenship	52	2.5 hrs.	multiple choice and open response

South Carolina

Exit-Level Exam: Basic Skills Assessment Program (**BSAP**) and Palmetto Achievement Challenge Tests (**PACT**)

State Education Department Website: www.myscschools.com/offices/assessment

Students take the BSAP in tenth grade and must pass all portions to graduate. Students may retake portions of the test once in eleventh grade and twice in the twelfth grade. The PACT will be given to tenth graders in the spring of 2004 and will test in English language arts, mathematics, and social studies.

Test	# Questions	Time	Question Type
BSAP Reading	60	untimed	multiple choice
BSAP Math	50	untimed	multiple choice
BSAP Writing	1	untimed	essay

Texas

Exit-Level Exam: Texas Assessment of Academic Skills (**TAAS**)

State Education Department Website: www.tea.state.tx.us

Students take the TAAS in tenth grade and must pass all three portions to graduate. Students have multiple opportunities to retake each portion of the exam.

Note that students who will be in the eleventh grade in spring 2004 or later and plan to graduate in spring 2005 or later will take a new test: the Texas Assessment of Knowledge and Skills (TAKS). This will cover English language arts, mathematics, science, and social studies.

Test	# Questions	Time	Question Type
Reading	40	untimed	multiple choice/essay
Writing	48	untimed	multiple choice/essay
Mathematics	60	untimed	multiple choice

Virginia

Exit-Level Exam: Standards of Learning (SOL)

State Education Department Website: www.pen.k12.va.us

Students must pass two SOL end-of-course English tests and any other four SOL end-of-course tests to graduate. Students entering ninth grade in 2003–04 must pass two English tests, one math test, one history test, one science test, and one test of their choosing in order to graduate. Students have multiple opportunities to retake portions of the exam.

The SOL tests are different from other exit-level exams in that there is no specific test for each subject area. Instead, numerous tests are offered in the required disciplines (i.e., biology and physics are tests offered in the science discipline). Listed below are the discipline areas where passing test scores are required for graduation.

Discipline Area	Time	Question Type
English	untimed	multiple choice and short answer
Math	untimed	multiple choice and short answer
Science	untimed	multiple choice and short answer
History & Social Sciences	untimed	multiple choice and short answer
Fine or Practical Arts	untimed	multiple choice and short answer
Health & Physical Education		
Electives		
Student Selected Test		

Washington

Exit-Level Exam: Washington Assessment of Student Learning (**WASL-10**)

State Education Department Website: www.k12.wa.us/assessment

Students take the WASL-10 in the tenth grade and are required to pass all subject-area tests to graduate. Students have multiple opportunities to retake portions of the exam. As of the 2003–04 school year, science will also be a required test.

Test	# Questions	Time	Question Type
Reading	40	untimed	multiple choice, short answers, extended answers
Math	42	untimed	multiple choice, short answers, extended answers
Writing	2	untimed	essay
Communication	8	untimed	multiple choice, short answers, extended answers

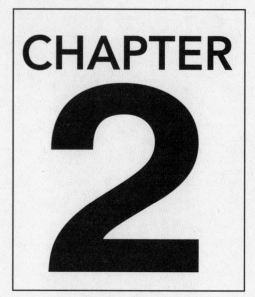

CHAPTER 2

TEST-TAKING TIPS AND STRATEGIES

Before you decide to skip this chapter and jump right into the grammar and writing sections, it's important to think about the entire preparation process. You need to make a study plan and stick to it, so you don't burn out too soon, or worse, end up cramming the night before the exam. You also need a plan for taking the actual test. Once you've got that in place, all you have to do on exam day is follow your plan in a calm, unstressed way.

Make a Study Plan

Hey, it's another test; you've seen them before. Studying for this test will be simpler and much more efficient if you figure out your situation and make a plan before you start. It should take you only a few minutes to make a study plan, but it will take loads of stress off you, so let's do it now.

First, figure out how many days you have between today and your exam day. Then subtract from that total the days you won't be able to study because of holidays, family obligations, or regular school exams or events.

Finally, figure out how much time you'll have to put in each day. You are the only one who knows exactly how much time it usually takes you to study for a regular test in school. If you've allowed yourself a month to review for the exam, you probably won't have to do more than 45 minutes to an hour every day, even if you need work in all subject areas of the exam. If, however, you only need to brush up your skills in one particular area, say essay writing, you may be able to reduce your study time to just 30 minutes a day.

The most important step in the study plan process is actually following the plan. Don't get so relaxed (or paralyzed by panic) about the test that you don't study a little every day. And, don't fall into the trap of thinking that you can spend 4 hours on Sunday night working exercises instead of doing them every day. It's much more effective to study for shorter periods every day than to do long sessions every now and then. Believe us, we know about these things.

Make a Test Day Plan

You can be incredibly well prepared because you made and stuck to your study plan, but if you're not prepared for the actual events of test day, your efforts will be wasted. The more you do to prepare for test day, the less that can go wrong. And if you're prepared for everything, you won't be as stressed out by anything minor that does happen.

> Chance favors the prepared mind. The more you do to prepare for things going wrong, the less likely it will be that anything will happen.

Location, Location, Location

Most state writing tests are given in your high school during the regular school day. However, some states reserve the right to schedule the test at a central location. Find out in advance where the test will be held. Double-check this information with your English teacher the day before the test. If, for any reason, the test will not be given at your school, make a dry run to the testing site at least once before test day. Your parents will be happy to do this if you point out that making a dry run will help you get a higher score on the test.

Think about how it would feel to be driving around in the car with your mom desperately looking for an unknown test location while you're supposed to be sitting down to take the test. Awful. Now, think about how great it would feel to breeze on in to the test with plenty of time to collect yourself before it starts.

Time

If the test is going to be given during the regular school day, you don't have to worry about time, since your teacher will probably herd the whole class to the cafeteria or wherever the test will be administered at the appropriate hour.

If the test administration falls on a day or time that conflicts with your religious observance, let your teacher know about this as far in advance as possible. She or he will be able to help you find out how you can get an alternate testing time.

The Night Before

It's probably pretty obvious that you shouldn't go out partying the night before the exam and come home an hour before you have to leave for school. But we're saying it anyway. On the other hand, you shouldn't spend the night before the test frantically cramming to try to soak up one last bit of information. In fact, cramming could actually hurt your performance on the test by causing anxiety and erasing some of the other stuff in your short-term memory (like what time the test starts).

A better use of your time the night before the test is to do something that relaxes you. Something that makes you laugh is even better. So rent a funny movie, watch it, and go to bed at a decent time. If you have trouble sleeping, try some of the relaxation techniques we mention in the Test Anxiety section below.

Know Your Enemy

Not all writing tests are the same. As soon as you can (but finish reading this page first!), you should find out exactly what the format of the writing test is in your state. On pages 3–12 of this book, we have provided a short guide to the state exams. Look under your state and you will find out the question types that you will encounter for each subject area. Check carefully to see whether you will have to deal with a multiple-choice section, a short-response section, and if you will need to write an essay.

Test Anxiety

> Test anxiety is like the sound of a buzzing mosquito in the middle of the dark. It can become so all-consuming that you forget what a tiny thing a mosquito bite really is.

Many students get positive results by using some relaxation techniques. One easy technique is called "observed breathing." Simply close your eyes and take note of your breaths in and out. Do not force the breath or change it in any way. Simply observe when you are taking air into your body and when you are expelling it. Stay quiet and observe your breathing for about 5 minutes. You should find that you'll start to feel a lot calmer.

In addition to relaxation techniques, there are more things you can do to control any anxiety you may have on test day.

Clothes

Dress in layers. You want to be able to put on clothes or strip down until you find the most comfortable temperature for you. You don't want your body to divert any of its thinking energy into shivering or sweating energy. And dress for comfort, not style. Sweats may not be your most flattering look, but sitting for a couple of hours in something tight or uncomfortable can have a negative effect on your performance.

Food and Drink

Eat breakfast the day of the test. A combination of protein and carbs will give you the energy you need to stay focused for several hours of testing. Eat eggs and oatmeal, bacon and toast, soba noodles with tofu, or whatever you like. Just stay away from lots of sugar, since you'll crash and burn right about the time you need to start writing.

Remember that if you drink a lot of liquids before the test, you need to get rid of them before you sit down to write. Make a pit stop before you go into the test room.

Your Mental State

Once you know you can write the essays and are physically comfortable during the test session, the only other factor to account for is your mental state. This is the trickiest aspect to have real control over, but it's also the one that can make all your preparation worthless if you don't manage it well. Try to keep your life in the week or so before the test as normal as possible. This way you won't have anything more pressing than the test to think about when you're actually taking the test. Intrigue about breaking up with your boyfriend or girlfriend or worrying about the friendship you just ended, your prom dress, or your summer vacation will do nothing but hurt your test score. So, try to keep everything as boring as possible so you can't help but focus on the test.

> The test itself is nothing but a few pieces of paper. Some of them have words written on them that you should read. The others are blank, and you have to write words on them.

If you've been doing relaxation exercises, take the time to do them on test day. If you find yourself freaking out right before or even during the test, put down your pencil, close your eyes, take a few deep breaths, and count or meditate. You'll lose a few minutes of your test time, but it's worth it to be calm and focused.

Ready for the fun to begin? Turn the page and start the grammar review.

PART

II

WRITING REVIEW

CHAPTER 3

GRAMMAR

What are the parts of speech in this sentence?

> *The drill sergeant and thirteen thin men marched silently across the desert.*

Though you probably haven't given much thought to English grammar in some time, you'll need to know a lot about it for the test. Grammar is tested in the multiple-choice sections, and it's also evaluated in the essays you write. So, before we identify all the parts of speech in that sentence above, here's the quick and dirty grammar review.

Parts of Speech

Every sentence you've ever written or spoken is made up of a number of specific **parts of speech**, which are the building blocks of the English language. The categories we're going to cover here are:

- nouns
- verbs
- adjectives
- adverbs
- prepositions
- conjunctions
- pronouns

The other parts of speech (like articles and interjections) aren't tested, so you shouldn't spend much time worrying about them.

Nouns

Nouns are words that refer to people, places, things, or ideas. Some examples are:

Alaska	*Robert*	*happiness*
school	*Harvey*	*freedom*
home	*Jennifer Lopez*	*liberty*

Nouns can be singular or plural. For example, *dog* is singular, while *dogs* is plural. Both are still nouns; only the quantity is different.

Proper Nouns

Proper nouns are names of *specific* people, places, or things, and they are always capitalized. Some examples are:

Madonna *World War II* *Findlay, Ohio*

GEE 21, Regents Exams, SOL, NCCT, AHSGE, GHSGT, BST, BSAP, WASL, CAHSEE, TAAS,
, WASL, CAHSEE, TAAS, OGT, HSPT/HSPA, FCAT, MEAP HST, MCAS, GEE 21, Regents Ex
Regents Exams, SOL, NCCT, AHSGE, GHSGT, BST, BSAP, WASL, CAHSEE

GRAMMAR

Common Nouns

Common nouns are general and don't refer to any specific person or thing. Some examples are:

> *singer*   *war*   *town*

Is Your Noun Countable?—Common nouns can be countable or uncountable. **Countable nouns** are, not surprisingly, tangible things that can be counted, like marbles, buildings, or candy bars. **Uncountable nouns** are usually intangible things (like traffic, humidity, or love) that can't be counted, but there are other uncountable tangible things, like soup or mashed potatoes. As we'll see, it's important to know if a noun is countable or not—especially when you're selecting a verb or adjective to go with that noun.

> Interestingly, "money" is an uncountable noun because it refers to one big amount and not a specific amount. "Dollars," however, is countable.

Can You Collect a Noun or Two?—**Collective nouns** usually refer to groups, and even though they comprise more than one item (for example, *family* means that you have more than one family member), the words are singular. We'll talk about this more when we get to subject-verb agreement.

Verbs

Verbs are words that describe actions or conditions in a sentence. Some examples of verbs are:

> *retires*   *go*   *chopped*   *had forgotten*   *will be*

Verb Tenses

In order to let the reader know when a specific action happened (the past), is happening (the present), or will happen (the future), verbs come in many tenses. The main three are the **present tense**, the **past tense**, and the **future tense**:

> The present: *I am President of the United States.*

> The past: *I was President of the United States.*

> The future: *I will be the President of the United States.*

When you write a sentence, it's important to keep the verb tense consistent. Otherwise, you might come up with something like this:

> *While Milo went to the grocery store, Denise will go to the mall.*

This sentence is awkward because most sentences refer to specific events as though they happened at the same time. The only time you should change tenses in a sentence is when it's absolutely necessary:

> *When I come back from pottery class, my sister will get her motorcycle repaired.*

ADJECTIVES

Adjectives modify nouns by providing more information about the noun. More than one adjective can modify a given noun. For example, in the phrase "long soft black fur," the adjectives *long*, *soft*, and *black* all modify *fur*.

Regular Adjectives (or How to Regulate Your Adjectives)

Regular adjectives provide more information about the noun they precede but do not compare that noun to any other. Some examples are *big* (i.e., "big dog"), *heartfelt* (i.e., "heartfelt request"), and *funny* (i.e., "funny story").

How Do Your Adjectives Compare?

Comparative adjectives compare the nouns they modify to other nouns. They either end in the letters *–er* or are preceded by the words *more* or *less*. Some examples are *bigger* (i.e., "a bigger dog"), *more heartfelt* (i.e., "a more heartfelt request"), or *less funny* (i.e., "a less funny story").

Superlative Adjectives (How Super Can They Be?)

Superlative adjectives compare the nouns they modify to other nouns. They either end in the letters *–est* or are preceded by the words *most* or *least*. Some examples are *biggest* (i.e., "the biggest dog"), *most heartfelt* (i.e., "the most heartfelt request"), or *least funny* (i.e., "the least funny story").

Comparatives and superlatives are used to compare two or more things. In fact, the number of things you're comparing tells you whether you should use a comparative (when you're talking about exactly two items) or a superlative (when you have three or more items).

Comparative	Superlative
older	*oldest*
more	*most*
less	*least*

📝 *Luis, the **older** of the two business partners, preferred backgammon to chess.*

📝 *Dorothy was the **oldest** of four sisters, so she was used to being in charge.*

Proper, Never Improper, Adjectives

Proper adjectives are a lot like proper nouns, since you're using the name of a person or place to describe something. All proper adjectives should also be capitalized:

Machiavellian scheme	*English* muffin
French pastries	*German* measles
Norman conquest	*Russian* dressing

NCCT, AHSGE GHSGT, BST, BSAP, WASL, CAHSEE, TAAS, OGT HSPA, FCAT, MEA
GT, HSPT/HSPA, FCAT, MEAP HST, MCAS, GEE21, Regents Exam NCCT, AHSGE, G

CHAPTER
3

There are a number of ordinary adjectives that have been derived from proper nouns. The word "quixotic," for example, comes from Cervantes's character, Don Quixote, who fought battles against imagined enemies.

ADVERBS

Adverbs modify verbs, adjectives, and other adverbs. Some examples are:

walked **slowly**	**hardly** noticeable
slept **soundly**	**so** poorly
really good	**really** well

Adjectives can often be turned into adverbs by adding an *–ly* to the adjective (or *–ally* on occasion). Some examples are:

stubborn → stubbornly

hopeful → hopefully

realistic → realistically

PREPOSITIONS

Prepositions connect words by telling how they relate to one another in space, time, or function. Some examples are:

The book is **on** the table.

The check is **in** the mail.

I lost my wallet **before** I got on the plane.

I chewed gum **as** I walked.

She sent me a card **for** my birthday.

You may be most familiar with prepositions as part of **prepositional phrases**, like "on the table," "in the mail," and "as I walked." These phrases serve the same purpose as adjectives because they add description to a sentence. For example:

☞ *I walked.* → becomes → *I walked **into the bowling alley**.*

In the prepositional phrase, "into the bowling alley," *into* is the preposition, *alley* is the object of the preposition, and *bowling* is an adjective to describe what type of alley it is.

It's possible to take a simple sentence and turn it into a really long one using a bunch of descriptive prepositional phrases:

The man lived. → becomes → The man [with a bright red moustache and a cute dog] lived [across the hall] [from the woman] [with the curly brown hair].

Single-Word and Phrasal Prepositions

Single-word prepositions are words like *on, in, around, behind, after,* etc. **Phrasal prepositions** are two- or three-word phrases that perform the function of a preposition, such as *because of, as of,* and *down through.*

Prepositions as Parts of Verb Phrases

Verbs are often paired up with a preposition to form a **verb phrase**. They are classified as part of the verb, not as prepositions on their own. It's important to know which prepositions go with which verbs. Some examples are:

call off	*hand in*	*come across*
turn up	*mull over*	*reckon with*

CHAPTER 3

Using the Right Preposition

As part of standard English usage, some words simply "go" with other words. These connections are part of what are called **idioms**. For most English idioms, using the right prepositions with the right verbs is important. A lot of grammar tests will also test your knowledge of idioms by how well you choose these prepositions:

- **Wrong:** *Most city dwellers regard raccoons like savage, slobbering garbage-eaters.*

- **Right:** *Most city dwellers regard raccoons* **as** *savage, slobbering garbage-eaters.*

Here are some examples of idiomatic usage of prepositions (see the **Idioms** section for more on this):

- *Decay is often the* **result of** *neglecting your teeth.*

- *Decay often* **results from** *neglecting your teeth.*

- *Neglecting your teeth often* **results in** *decay.*

> Different languages have different idioms. For example, in English, we say "I am hungry." The phrase that means the same thing in French is, "J'ai faim," which literally means "I have hunger" in English.

Prepositional Phrases

Prepositional phrases are made of a preposition followed by a noun phrase or gerund.

GRAMMAR

A noun phrase is simply a noun with an article or pronoun in front of it (to indicate how many of the noun there is and whether the noun is specific or non-specific) and maybe one or more adjectives that describe it further. For example, "the big dog" is a noun phrase and so is "my dilapidated old red jalopy."

Some examples of prepositional phrases are:

behind the old tree stump   *out of* all the contestants

because of his peanut allergy   *in* the lake

Each of these phrases begins with a preposition (*behind, because of, out of,* or *in*) and ends with a noun phrase ("the old tree stump," "his peanut allergy," "all the contestants," or "the lake").

A prepositional phrase cannot be broken up by other words, and it can never be a sentence on its own (because it doesn't have a subject or a verb).

Prepositional phrases serve the same function as adverbs and adjectives in that they modify the rest of the sentence. For example, let's look at the following sentence:

> *Hockey games* **in Canada** *make more revenue for the television networks that broadcast them than do hockey games in the United States.*

In this example, the prepositional phrase "in Canada" acts as an adjective because it describes the noun phrase "hockey games," not the verb *make*. However, the same prepositional phrase can also act like an adverb. Let's look at another sentence.

> *The holiday of Thanksgiving occurs in October* **in Canada***.*

In this sentence, the prepositional phrase "in Canada" modifies the verb *occurs* by telling us where the holiday of Thanksgiving occurs. Therefore, it acts like an adverb in this case.

> Prepositional phrases can make the difference between an ambiguous sentence ("No one eats bagels") and a clear one ("No one in my family eats bagels from Abel's Bagels during the week").

CONJUNCTIONS (WHAT'S THEIR FUNCTION?)

Conjunctions connect words, phrases, or clauses to each other. Some examples are:

- ☞ *Romeo **and** Juliet*
- ☞ *You like coffee, **but** I like tea.*
- ☞ *I ate the pie, **although** gooseberry isn't my favorite flavor.*
- ☞ *I could eat an apple **or** an orange.*
- ☞ *That store sells neither postcards **nor** electric razors.*

Parts of a Sentence

Parts of a sentence are the units that create a sentence. Each part can consist of one word or a group of words that go together. The parts of a sentence that we're going to cover are prepositional phrases, verbs (including action verbs and linking verbs), subjects, direct objects, indirect objects, predicate words, and compound parts.

SUBJECTS

The **subject** of a sentence is the part that refers to the person, place, or thing that performs the main action in the sentence. It usually appears first in the sentence.

The subject can be a single word, a phrase, or multiple phrases. An example of a sentence with a single-word subject is:

☞ *Justin ate a ham sandwich.*

Examples of sentences with subjects consisting of a phrase are:

☞ **The huge, kidney-shaped swimming pool** *was filled with Hawaiian Punch.*

☞ **My mother** *gave me $20.*

☞ **Her ex-boyfriend, Raul,** *used to be a professional dance instructor.*

In these sentences, "huge, kidney-shaped swimming pool," "my mother," and "her ex-boyfriend, Raul" are all subjects consisting of a phrase.

Examples of sentences with subjects consisting of more than one phrase are:

☞ **The red car she bought when she was 18** *is still parked in her parents' garage.*

☞ **Everyone who came to the concert without a ticket** *had to pay an extra fee at the entrance.*

In these sentences, the bold phrases are subjects consisting of more than one phrase.

What's Really Going On?

Don't be fooled into thinking that the subject of a sentence has to be short or that a subject can't contain a verb. For example:

> *The red car she bought when she was 18 is still parked in her parents' garage.*

In this example, the verb *bought* isn't the verb that describes the action of the sentence. Instead, it's just part of a clause that gives us more information about the red car. The verb that describes the action of the sentence is *is*. Here's another example:

> *Everyone who came to the concert without a ticket had to pay an extra fee at the entrance.*

In the same way, the verb *came* is part of a clause that gives us more information about *everyone*. The verb that describes the action of the sentence is *had to pay*.

Compound Subjects

The simple sentence "Justin ate a ham sandwich" has one subject, but you can have as many subject nouns as you want in a sentence, which we call a **compound subject**. For example:

> *Justin, Margaret, Inez, the mailman, and the mailman's cousin Trudy ate a ham sandwich.*

> If you've read this far all in one sitting, your eyes might be glazing over by now. Take a break. Go get a glass of water, take a walk around the block, or ask your mom how her day was (and then listen to her answer). Then, come back and read the rest of this chapter.

THE PREDICATE

The second half of a sentence is often referred to as the **predicate,** and it usually includes the verb and whatever objects are used.

> Justin *ate a ham sandwich.*

It's just as possible to have a compound subject as it is to have a **compound predicate.**

> Justin *ate a ham sandwich, four apples, and a gallon of pistachio ice cream.*

Objects

Just as subject nouns commit the action, **object nouns** receive it. In other words, object nouns are the items to which something is done:

> Marcus washed **the car.**

There can also be many objects in one sentence:

> Marcus washed the **car,** his **clothes,** his **face,** and the **dog.**

Each of the bold words in the previous sentence is a **direct object** because each directly receives the action (all of them were washed). However, there's also such a thing as an **indirect object,** which isn't the main object of the sentence but still factors into its construction. For example:

> All that jackhammering gave **me** a headache.

The direct object of the sentence is *headache,* and *me* is the indirect object.

Agreement of Subject and Verb (Agree to Agree)

When you construct a sentence, the noun and the verb have to agree; that is, if the noun is singular, then the verb has to be singular as well. Likewise, plural nouns go with plural verbs.

Also, remember that a compound subject should be treated like a plural subject:

> **Wrong:** *My mother and I is going to learn Spanish.*

> **Right:** *My mother and I **are** going to learn Spanish.*

PT/HSPA, FCAT, MEAP HST, MCAS, GEE21, Regents Exams, SOL, NCCT, AHSGE, GHSGT,
NCCT, AHSGE, GHSGT, BST, BSAP, WASL, CAHSEE, TAAS, OGT, T/HSPA, FCAT, MEA
GT, HSPT/HSPA, FCAT, MEAP HST, MCAS, GEE21, Regents Exams, NCCT, AHSGE, G

CHAPTER
3

Collective Nouns (**Pass the Hat!**)—As stated earlier in the chapter, **collective nouns** are words for groups of things that sound plural but are really singular. The example we gave was the word *family,* which is a singular noun that means a collection of individuals related to one another. Other examples are *team, group,* and *herd.* It's important to choose a singular verb to go with them. Some examples are:

☑ *The team of cheerleaders* **is** *getting on the bus.*

☑ *A family of five* **eats** *a lot more now than it did fifty years ago.*

☑ *That herd of buffalo* **is** *stampeding toward the river.*

☑ *I wonder if that group of seagulls* **knows** *that the tide is going out.*

Double Negatives (or Don't Do Nothing That We Wouldn't Do)

When you want to make a verb negative, be sure only to add one negative word to the sentence:

☑ *I want candy.* → becomes → *I* **don't** *want candy.*

If you add more than one negative word, they will cancel each other out:

☑ *I* **don't** *want* **no** *candy.*

Sentences like these are called **double negatives**, and it's important (both in life and for the purposes of this test) that you not use them.

Pronouns

Teacher: "Quick. Give me two pronouns."

Student: "Who, me?"

We'd all be out of breath if we had to refer to the same noun over and over again:

☑ *While Dennis was on Dennis's way to Dennis's grandmother's house with Dennis's mom, Dennis's mom scolded Dennis for making faces at Dennis's mom.*

Pronouns are a great way for us to use a type of shorthand when referring to nouns:

> *While Dennis was on **his** way to **his** grandmother's house with **his** mom, **she** scolded **him** for making faces at **her**.*

As you might expect, there are a lot of different pronouns that are used in specific circumstances.

Pronouns are the parts of speech that give students the most trouble. That's why we've using so much space to cover them thoroughly.

Subject and Object Pronouns

Lots of English tests like to trick you when it comes to pronouns because some students have difficulty deciding which pronoun to use. If you get confused, remember that the pronoun you use depends on what the noun in the sentence is doing. If the original noun is committing the action, use a **subject pronoun**:

> *After Vladimir got home from school, **he** started cleaning his room.*

Conversely, object nouns should be replaced by **object pronouns**:

> *After Vladimir got home from school, his mother told **him** to clean his room.*

How would you respond to a sentence like this?

> *Me and **him** saw a ghost at the library last week.*

This sentence is wrong because even though the pronouns are clearly doing the action, the pronouns being used are object pronouns. The correct sentence reads:

> *He and I saw a ghost at the library last week.*

Subject Pronouns	Object Pronouns
I	me
you	you
he/she/it	him/her/it
we	us
you	you
they	them

Other Pronouns

There are many words we use all the time that you might not have realized are actually pronouns. Examples include:

- *Bananas, **which** are high in potassium, are an excellent snack.*

- *The guy **who** dated my sister moved to Phoenix.*

- *The goose **that** laid the golden egg escaped to a bird sanctuary.*

- *Al Capone was **one** of the most notorious criminals ever known.*

In each of these cases, the bolded word is referring to the noun that preceded it.

Making Pronouns Agree

There are two main rules for using pronouns:

1. Each pronoun has to agree with the noun it is replacing.

    If the original noun is singular, then the pronoun should be singular as well:

    - **Wrong:** *When Janine was sick, **they** stayed home from school.*
    - **Right:** *When Janine was sick, **she** stayed home from school.*

    The same holds true for plural nouns, which need to be re-placed with plural pronouns:

    - **Wrong:** *Cats sometimes act so strangely, it's impossible to understand it.*
    - **Right:** *Cats sometimes act so strangely, it's impossible to understand them.*

2. Each pronoun must refer directly to the noun it is replacing.

    - *When I saw Ned and Michael at the swimming pool, I went over to talk to him.*

    There's a problem here. Will the narrator go talk to Ned or Michael? *Him* is an improper, or ambiguous, pronoun that needs to be replaced in one of two ways:

    - *When I saw Ned and Michael at the swimming pool, I went over to talk to **them**.*

OR

☞ *When I saw Ned and Michael at the swimming pool, I went over to talk to **Ned/Michael**.*

Either way (and depending on what the narrator wants to say), the meaning of the sentence is now clear.

So, Does Your Pronoun Agree? (It don't, does it?)—It's important to make sure that the "other pronouns" agree with their verbs as well. If you're not sure whether a pronoun is singular or plural, try this test: Can you add the word *one* to the sentence? For example:

☞ ***Each** of the students are going to pass the physics test.*

This sentence is incorrectly worded because *each* is a singular pronoun. You can tell because if you can add *one* to the sentence, it still makes sense:

☞ *Each **one** of the students are going to pass the physics test.*

Therefore, a singular pronoun needs a singular verb, and the proper way to write this sentence is like this:

☞ *Each of the students **is** going to pass the physics test.*

Examples of other singular pronouns include:

either	*neither*
every	*none (not one)*

"Each" and "neither" are often paired with prepositional phrases:
☞ Each [of the man's forty-nine spectacular racehorses] is [in the stable].
☞ Neither [of the cats] is interested in playing [with the ball] [of string].

CHAPTER 3

Who vs. Whom

The *who/whom* conundrum can be a real head-scratcher. We use both to tell people that we don't know the identity of a specific person ("Halt! Who goes there?"), but when are you supposed to use which one? Luckily, there is a very clear distinction: *Who* is a subject pronoun, and *whom* is an object pronoun. Use *who* when the unknown person is committing an action:

> **Who** *keeps making those terrible noises?*

Use *whom* when the unknown person is receiving the action:

> *After I get the ball, to* **whom** *should I pass it?*

There's a great little rule to help you remember this. If the answer to the question is *he* or *she* (subject pronouns), use *who*. If the answer is *him* or *her* (object pronouns), use *whom*.

> **Who** *keeps making those terrible noises?*   Answer: **He** *does.*

> *After I get the ball, to* **whom** *should I pass it?*   Answer: *Pass it to* **her**.

> If you're still a little wary of the who vs. whom dilemma, just don't use any questions in your essay, and you'll probably be able to avoid it altogether.

Adjectives and Adverbs

We rely on **adverbs** and **adjectives** to make our sentences more descriptive.

> *The fox jumped over the dog.*

becomes

> *The* **quick, brown** *fox* **lightly** *jumped over the* **lazy** *dog.*

You've added a bunch of descriptive words, and the sentence now gives the reader a lot more information. In many ways, the best writing uses well-chosen descriptive words to convey vivid images to the reader. And of course, the better your vocabulary is, the better your word choice will be.

WRITING

☞ *The **swift, auburn** fox **nimbly** jumped over the **indolent** dog.*

Swift, *auburn*, and *indolent* are all adjectives that describe nouns (the fox and the dog). But *nimbly* is an adverb that describes the verb *jump*. Writers often use adverbs, which often end in *–ly*, to describe action verbs. For example:

☞ *The doctor responded **alertly** to the distress call.*

When someone asks you how you feel, do you say "I feel good" or "I feel well"? The correct answer (assuming you're not sick) is that you feel good. Since *well* is an adverb, saying that you feel well means that you are good at feeling things, not that there's nothing wrong with you.

Adverbs with Adjectives—Adverbs can also be used to add further description to adjectives.

☞ *I was **barely** awake when the phone rang.*

Awake is an adjective, or descriptive term, to describe the subject, *I*, and *barely* adds more description by telling us *how* awake he or she was.

Punctuation

End Marks

The most common way to end a sentence is with a **period**. Like there. And that one also. Periods are the best way to tell someone, "OK, you can stop now." Of course, periods are kind of bland, and they don't tell you if there's any emotion involved in the sentence.

If a sentence is an interrogative (in other words, a question), use a question mark:

☞ *Do you know the way to San Jose?*

To convey to the reader that someone was yelling or otherwise raising his voice, use an exclamation point:

  Of course I know the way to San Jose!

> You will probably not need to use any exclamation points in your essay. It is not considered good writing to use exclamation points unless they are part of a quote or dialogue. Using them in an essay makes you sound like an infomercial. Just say no to exclamation points! (See what we mean?)

Commas

A **comma**, unlike a period, is merely used as a brief pausing point between two words. Many times two commas are used to set off a descriptive word or phrase from the rest of the sentence. It's important to note that this phrase has nothing to do with the noun-verb setup of the sentence; in fact, you should be able to take it out of the sentence without affecting its construction. For example:

  Before: *My dad ate the last Twinkie.*

  After: *My dad, **a handsome carpenter in his late 50s**, ate the last Twinkie.*

Commas are also used to set off the two parts of a compound sentence. For example, you can join the sentences "Koala bears like Eucalyptus leaves" and "I don't particularly care for them" by using a conjunction and a comma:

  *Koala bears like Eucalyptus leaves, **but** I don't particularly care for them.*

Note that both parts of the compound sentence are complete sentences that can stand alone. Only place a comma before a conjunction when you are joining two complete sentences. For example:

  Wrong: *Koala bears like Eucalyptus leaves, and are often very drowsy.*

  Right: *Koala bears like Eucalyptus leaves and are often very drowsy.*

You should also use a comma right before you quote what somebody said:

> *Marisol shrieked, "Who has been playing my Frank Sinatra albums?"*

Apart from these examples, commas are most commonly used to indicate to the reader that he or she should take a breath. As you read other texts, take a look at where commas are used.

> Be careful not to use a comma when you should use a semicolon. If the two sentences are complete, you can only join them with a comma if you also use a conjunction.

Apostrophes

> *At 12 o'clock on Halloween, Mary's sister couldn't find her friend's bag of candy.*

An **apostrophe** stands in for a letter or letters that have been removed from a word. The most common use of apostrophes is for **contractions**—when two words have been crammed (or contracted) into one.

Source	Contraction
will not	won't
are not	aren't
she is	she's
you are	you're
I am	I'm
I will	I'll
I would	I'd

The next-most-common use is for **possessives**, or when you want to indicate that something belongs to someone (the apostrophe is usually followed by an *s*):

> *Jimmy's sweater*

> *Your father's Oldsmobile*

> *Winona County's many voters*

T/HSPA, FCAT, MEAP HST, MCAS, GEE21, Regents Exams, SOL, AHSGE, GHSGT,
NCCT, AHSGE, GHSGT, BST, BSAP, WASL, CAHSEE, TAAS, OGT, HSPA, FCAT, MEA
T, HSPT/HSPA, FCAT, MEAP HST, MCAS, GEE21, Regents Exams, NCCT, AHSGE, G

CHAPTER 3

There are other examples where apostrophes are used, like in the examples on the previous page. The term "o'clock" is short for "of the clock," but we use the apostrophe to shorten that phrase down a little. Similarly, "Hallowe'en" is really a short version of "hallowed evening," but we've been saying Halloween for so long that the apostrophe isn't used much anymore.

Other Notes about Using an Apostrophe—If a singular noun already ends in *s*, be sure to add another *s* after the apostrophe:

> *When Thomas Jefferson became president in 1801, he took John **Adams's** place.*

If you have a plural noun that you want to make possessive, the apostrophe goes on the outside of the *s*:

> *The **hikers'** view of the mountain was blocked by a huge cloud of fog.*

Colons

Colons are used most of the time to indicate that a list is coming. For example:

> *The following companies make cool cars: Porsche, Ferrari, and Lamborghini.*

Another way to use a colon is to set apart a question from the rest of a sentence:

> *Now that the "X-Files" series has ended, industry watchers are asking: What is David Duchovny up to now?*

Don't confuse colons and semi-colons. Colons are only used for lists or to set off questions; semi-colons are only used to connect two sentences.

Semi-Colons

You can attach two simple sentences together by using a **semi-colon**. However, the sentences must be complete; never use sentence fragments.

☞ **Wrong:** *People don't understand the badger; such a nice animal.*

☞ **Right:** *People don't understand the badger; **it's** such a nice animal.*

You can tell that you used the semi-colon correctly because each of the phrases on either side of the semi-colon can be used as a complete sentence by itself.

Idiom List

Here's a list of some of the idioms that most English-speaking high school students should know (though it isn't a comprehensive list of every idiom on the planet). Whenever you see an idiom for the first time, add it to this list and memorize it so you can use it and recognize it in the future.

> Idioms are often the most difficult things to learn when you are learning a foreign language because sometimes they don't make much sense. If you think about it, why do we say "according to" and not "according from"? If English is not your first language, you should be extra diligent about studying this list. Even if it is your first language, pay close attention so that you don't misuse an idiom.

able to, ability to
> *Grandpa is no longer able to juggle chainsaws the way he used to.*
> *Turtles have the ability to sleep in their shells for weeks at a time.*

access to
> *During the scandal, reporters were not given access to secret files.*

according to
> *According to government sources, cheddar cheese is a very nutritious snack.*

account for
> *France accounts for 70 percent of all red wine made throughout the world.*

NCCT, AHSGE, GHSGT, BST, BSAP, WASL, CAHSEE, TAAS, OGT, HSPA, FCAT, ME
OGT, HSPT/HSPA, FCAT, MEAP HST, MCAS, GEE21, Regents Exam NCCT, AHSGE, G

CHAPTER
3

WRITING

accuse of

> *During the war, Private Benjamin was accused of treason.*

agree with

> *I don't agree with your opinion.*

appear to

> *People who live in big cities often don't appear to be very friendly.*

apply to

> *I'm going to apply to fifteen colleges this spring.*

argue over

> *The roommates always argued over whose turn it was to wash the dishes.*

as [adjective] as

> *My uncle is as smart as most nuclear physicists.*

assure that

> *I assure you that I have never eaten a blueberry Pop Tart.*

at a disadvantage

> *For many teenagers, living in poverty puts them at a disadvantage in school.*

attempt to

> *The pole vaulter attempted to clear 15 feet.*

attend to, attention to

> *Baby-sitters don't always attend to children as well as they should.*
> *The accountant was known for his attention to detail.*

attribute to

> *Many clever quotes are attributed to Mark Twain.*

available to

> *Is your aunt available to baby-sit on Friday night?*

based on

> *The play was based on a true story.*

because of

> *Because of the time difference, she had to call Paris at 3 a.m.*

believed to be

> *He is believed to be the only living descendant of George Washington.*

between [1] and [2]

> *Just between you and me, I think that movie was really bad.*

call for

> Old King Cole called for three fiddlers.

choice of

> The airplane passengers were given a choice of chicken or fish for dinner.

choose to [verb]

> Many people choose to attend vocational school rather than a four-year college.

choose from [nouns]

> Students were offered the chance to choose from dozens of different science classes.

claim to

> My cousin's claim to fame is that he once delivered a pizza to Robert De Niro.

considered or **considered to be**

> Picasso is considered one of the world's finest abstract painters.
> Picasso is considered to be one of the world's finest abstract painters.

consist of

> The project consists of a paper, an oral presentation, and a scale model.

consistent with

> The results of my experiment were consistent with those of my lab partner.

continue to

> I called the police because my neighbor continued to play his stereo at top volume at 3 in the morning.

contrast with

> Her wild dress and hip boots really contrasted with her date's polo shirt and khakis.

contribute to

> We asked our Home Ec teacher to contribute to our tenth grade bake sale.

cost of [something]

> The cost of a Big Mac is used to compare the rate of inflation.

cost to [someone]

> If you order now, we'll throw in a bottle of our special Lime Juice Miracle, at no cost to you!

credit with

> I'd like to credit my mother with teaching me how to whistle.

deal with

>   When I got home from school, the last thing I wanted to deal with was bubble gum on my shoes.

debate over

>   The debate over whether or not our school should start an hour earlier caused a riot at the school board meeting.

decide to (not decide on)

>   "We've decided to turn your room into a home gym as soon as you leave for college," my parents announced gleefully.

defend against

>   Atlanta tried to defend itself against Sherman's attack without success.

define as

>   Nationalism is defined as loyalty and devotion to a nation, according to Merriam-Webster's Collegiate Dictionary.

delighted by

>   I was delighted by the grade I received on my final exam in chemistry class.

demonstrate that

>   I used some coffee and some grape juice to demonstrate that Lime Juice Miracle can remove any stain from carpet.

depend on

>   Which college I attend depends on which colleges accept me.

descend from

>   The trapeze artist descended from the ceiling on a swing.

different from

>   My aspirations for the future are different from yours—I want to be a trapeze artist and you want to be an American idol.

difficult to

>   It is difficult to concentrate on my geometry homework when I can smell peach cobbler baking in the kitchen.

distinguish [1] from [2]

>   "I think I might be colorblind," said my brother. "I can't distinguish green from red."

draw on

>   She drew on all her years of experience as a teacher to get us to learn the words to "How Deep Is Your Love" in Spanish.

due to

> *Due to a scheduling error, our homecoming game was an away game.*

[in an] effort to

> *In an effort to preserve water, the town council mandated a rule that residents could only water their lawns in the rain.*

either…or

> *"Either I go or he goes!" my father shouted, pointing at my hamster.*

encourage to

> *I encourage you to stay in school instead of dropping out.*

–er than (taller than, bigger than, smarter than, etc.)

> *I am taller than anyone else in my gym class.*

estimate to be

> *She is estimated to be older than 90, although no one knows for sure.*

expose to

> *I was exposed to chicken pox three times before I finally caught it.*

extent of

> *We only found out the extent of her obsession with marbles after she died and we could look in her closets.*

fear that

> *She feared that if she wore the same shoes two days in a row no one would be her friend.*

forbid to

> *"I forbid you to leave this house in that outfit!" screamed my mother.*

force to

> *I had to force myself to eat the horrible-tasting cake at my birthday party.*

frequency of

> *We discovered that the frequency of air conditioner thefts increased during the heat wave last year.*

from [1] to [2]

> *I changed my ticket from today to Wednesday so I could go to the amusement park with my class.*

in contrast to

> *In contrast to her previous boyfriend, her current boyfriend wore shoes when he was in public.*

in danger of

> *He was in danger of causing a traffic accident when he walked around with no shirt on.*

in order to

> *In order to graduate from high school, you have to pass your exit-level exam.*

inclined to

> *I am not inclined to believe him after all the lies he told me about his family.*

infected with

> *Once I was infected with chicken pox, I didn't know why I wanted to get it in the first place.*

instead of

> *Instead of riding the bus to school, she decided to walk.*

introduce to

> *My grandfather introduced me to his best friend from grade school.*

isolate from

> *Students with learning disabilities sometimes feel isolated from everyone else in their classes.*

just as . . . so too

> *Just as my parents grew up and got boring, so too will my sister some day.*

less than

> *Even though she finished less than one half of the book, she still wrote a B+ book report.*

likely to (also unlikely to)

> *I did not think she was likely to go to the prom with me after I tripped and spilled spaghetti sauce on her white blouse.*

mistake for

> *You would never mistake me for a graceful ballet dancer.*

more than

> *My cousin ate more pies than anyone else at the county fair.*

move away from

> *My sister couldn't wait to move away from home, but now she comes over every night for dinner.*

native to or a native of

> *This plant is native to Wyoming.*
> *My teacher is a native of Wyoming, but she had never seen the plant before.*

neither . . . nor

She ordered neither maple syrup nor chocolate sauce with her Belgian waffles.

not [1] but [2]

Not love but jealousy drove him to marry someone he'd only known for eight days.

not only . . . but also

He is not only a wonderful singer but also a black belt in karate.

on account of

We hid in the basement for 3 hours on account of the tornado warning.

opportunity for [noun]

"This seems like a perfect opportunity for mischief," said the teacher when she noticed that the gate was unlocked.

opportunity to [verb]

Whenever you have the opportunity to eat key lime pie, you should, in my opinion.

opposed to

I am opposed to any form of violence as discipline for children.

opposite of

The opposite of black is white.

permit to

The woman was not permitted to enter the deli with her poodle.

persuade to

It took all the ice cream in my freezer to persuade my friend to tell me the secret.

pressure to

Bruce Springsteen felt pressure to play all his old songs on his concert tour even though he was more interested in his new ones.

prevent from

Air bags are meant to prevent you from being injured in an auto accident.

prized by

Prized by collectors, the rare first edition of the book was the only thing the thieves stole.

prohibit from

Poodles are prohibited from entering delis.

protect against

> A good hair conditioner can help protect against split ends.

provide with

> My parents provided me with love, food, clothes, and a warm house, but not a Corvette on my sixteenth birthday.

question whether

> Have you ever questioned whether you will ever be done with studying?

range from [1] to [2]

> The judges' scores on her ice skating performance ranged from 4.4 to 5.9.

rather than

> My father would rather eat vegetables than meat.

regard as

> Dr. Pantley is regarded as the foremost expert in her field.

replace with

> We've secretly replaced this fine gourmet coffee with Folger's Crystals.

require of and **require to**

> My school requires 40 hours of community service a year from each student.
> We are required to do community service if we want to graduate.

responsibility to

> My friend has the responsibility to train for a marathon.

responsible for

> She is responsible for running a certain number of miles every day.

result from and **result in**

> Her success in running the marathon will result from her consistent training.
> All the miles she runs will result in a great time in the marathon.

the same as

> My school schedule is the same as yours this year.

see as

> We all see Ms. Carter as the best teacher in the school.

send to

> My grandmother sent a package to me at camp this summer.

sense of

> Her sense of style increased after she started reading Vogue magazine.

so. . .that

> She is so pretty that she makes guys nervous.

spend on

> If you start investing the money you spend on cheeseburgers each year, you could retire when you're 40.

subject to

> The money you win in the lottery is subject to taxes, unfortunately.

substitute [1] for [2]

> I substituted baking soda for baking powder in the cake recipe, and it came out as flat as a pancake.

suffer from

> She suffered from a broken heart for exactly two days until she met her new boyfriend.

superior to

> As soon as I got my driver's license I felt superior to my brother, who was still too young to drive.

suspicious of

> My mother was suspicious of the man behind her in line at the ATM because he kept trying to see the buttons she was pressing.

targeted at

> The Saturday morning cartoon commercials are targeted at children who can convince their parents to buy them lots of toys.

the –er, the –er

> The bigger the foot, the higher the shoe size.

the use of

> The use of illegal drugs is strictly prohibited during the summer program.

the way to [verb] is to [verb]

> The way to walk confidently is to hold your head high and your shoulders back.

think of. . .as

> I think of him as a role model.

threaten to

> My mother threatened to take away my Playstation if I got another C in algebra.

train to

> Despite my best efforts, I could never train my cat to bring me a can of soda.

CHAPTER 3

transmit to

> *Once the head office tallied the results, it transmitted them to all the local offices.*

try to

> *Our assignment was to try to drop an egg from a third-floor window without breaking it.*

type of

> *What type of girls do you usually go out with?*

use as

> *She forgot her purse, so she had to use her sleeve as a tissue.*

view as

> *I viewed her comment that my dress was "so retro" as an insult.*

vote for

> *It is your duty to vote for the candidate who you think best espouses your views.*

willing to/unwilling to

> *I was not willing to give up sleeping in on Saturday mornings, so I quit the team.*
> *I was unwilling to sell my baseball card collection to a collector.*

worry about

> *If you worry about the writing test too much, you will give yourself an ulcer.*

All Together Now

Let's go back to that first sentence that was at the beginning of the chapter:

> *The drill sergeant and the thirteen thin men in his platoon marched silently across the desert.*

What are the parts of speech?

Word	Part of speech
The	definite article (don't worry about this one)
drill sergeant	noun (subject)
and	conjunction
thirteen, thin	adjectives
men	plural noun (subject)
marched	verb
silently	adverb
across the desert	prepositional phrase

Now that you've read the whole chapter, identifying the parts of speech of the sentence should be entirely doable, if not a snap.

Pop Quiz

Directions: Questions 1–7 refer to the following paragraph. Read the paragraph, and then answer the questions that follow.

(1) I don't hardly ever get to visit my best friend. (2) I really like going to visit her. (3) Its always fun when we spend time together. (4) Me and her always go to the beach. (5) We where bathing suits and swim in the ocean. (6) Sometimes we see fish in the see. (7) I wish I was at the beach now.

1. Sentence 1: I don't hardly ever get to visit my best friend.
   What correction should be made to this sentence?

   (A) change <u>don't</u> to <u>do not</u>

   (B) delete <u>don't</u>

   (C) delete <u>hardly</u>

   (D) No correction is necessary.

2. Sentence 2: I really like going to visit her often.
   What correction should be made to this sentence?

   (F) delete <u>going</u>

   (G) change <u>to</u> to <u>too</u>

   (H) delete <u>often</u>

   (J) No correction is necessary.

3. Sentence 3: Its always fun when we spend time together.
   What correction should be made to this sentence?

   (A) change <u>Its</u> to <u>It's</u>

   (B) replace <u>always</u> with <u>all ways</u>

(C) change <u>when</u> to <u>win</u>

     (D) No correction is necessary.

4. Sentence 4: Me and her always go to the beach.
   What correction should be made to this sentence?

     (F) change <u>Me and her</u> to <u>She and me</u>

     (G) change <u>Me and her</u> to <u>She and I</u>

     (H) change <u>Me and her</u> to <u>I and her</u>

     (J) No correction is necessary.

5. Sentence 5: We where bathing suits and swim in the ocean.
   What correction should be made to this sentence?

     (A) change <u>where</u> to <u>wear</u>

     (B) change <u>where</u> to <u>were</u>

     (C) change <u>bathing suits</u> to <u>bathingsuits</u>

     (D) No correction is necessary.

6. Sentence 6: Sometimes we see fish in the see.
   What correction should be made to this sentence?

     (F) change the first <u>see</u> to <u>sea</u>

     (G) change <u>Sometimes</u> to <u>Some times</u>

     (H) change the second <u>see</u> to <u>sea</u>

     (J) No correction is necessary.

7. Sentence 7: I wish I was at the beach now.
   What correction should be made to this sentence?

     (A) end the sentence with a question mark

     (B) change <u>was</u> to <u>were</u>

     (C) change <u>now</u> to <u>know</u>

     (D) No correction is necessary.

Answers and Explanations

1. **The correct answer is (B).** The word <u>don't</u> sets up a double negative, which is ungrammatical and weakens the sentence.

2. **The correct answer is (F).** In this sentence, the word <u>going</u> used with <u>to visit</u> is poor grammar.

3. **The correct answer is (A).** <u>It's</u> is the contraction for <u>It is</u>.

4. **The correct answer is (G).** The compound subject of the sentence should be in the subjective case instead of the objective case.

5. **The correct answer is (A).** The correct word to use is the verb <u>wear</u> instead of its homonym <u>where</u>.

6. **The correct answer is (H).** The correct word is <u>sea</u> instead of its homonym <u>see</u>.

7. **The correct answer is (B).** The correct tense of the verb is <u>were</u> instead of <u>was</u>.

CHAPTER 4

MULTIPLE-CHOICE QUESTIONS

In this section, we'll talk about the best way for you to work through and answer the multiple-choice questions on the writing test. We'll talk about the process of elimination (the most important technique you can use), and then we'll describe the types of passages you will see and the types of questions you'll be asked.

Process of Elimination

One of the best ways to get the correct answers on the multiple-choice section of the writing test, or on any multiple-choice test, is to use the **process of elimination** to help you find the correct answer. In essence, you should be looking for the incorrect answers instead of the correct one. This may seem a bit backward, but it's actually easier and more likely to lead you to the correct answer.

Think of it this way: If you can eliminate all the things that you know are wrong, even if you have more than one answer choice left, you've seriously increased the odds of choosing the correct answer, even if you guess blindly. Let's see how it works:

> **Example:** Ana Maria moved <u>her</u> clothes back to Washington once the school year was over.
>
> Which part of speech is the underlined word in the sentence above?
>
> **(A)** Subject pronoun
>
> **(B)** Object pronoun
>
> **(C)** Conjunction
>
> **(D)** Predicate noun

If you just blindly guessed at the answer to this question, you'd have a 25 percent chance of getting it right, because 1 out of the 4 answer choices is correct, and 1 out of 4 is 25 percent. Let's see if we can eliminate any of the answer choices. The word is *her*, which you should recognize as a pronoun. (If you don't, go back and review Chapter 3 again.) Even if you don't recognize it immediately as a pronoun, you should at least be able to tell that it isn't a conjunction (like *and* or *but*), so eliminate answer choice (C). It's also not a noun, predicate or otherwise, so eliminate answer choice (D). Now you're left with choices (A) and (B). Even if you didn't go any farther and just guessed from between these two answer choices, you've increased your odds of getting the correct answer to 50 percent. That's a huge increase.

By the way, the correct answer is (B). "Her" is an object pronoun. The corresponding subject pronoun is "she."

There is no way you can lose by using process of elimination. It may seem slow and cumbersome to you at first, but once you've practiced it on the questions at the end of this book you'll be able to use it quickly and accurately.

The Passages

Most of the multiple-choice questions you will see on the writing test will be based on one of several types of written passages. Let's talk about the passages and how to navigate them efficiently.

Long Papers

These passages will be long papers (2–3 pages) that fictitious students have written for class. Each paper may be a personal essay or a research paper. Each sentence will be numbered, and there will be grammatical mistakes in the paper. Your task will be to answer questions asking about the purpose or intent of the paper, or asking you to suggest changes that would improve the paper. The changes could be grammatical, but they could also ask you to rearrange the sentences or to add or delete sentences to change the meaning or flow of the paper.

Sections of Papers

These will be short passages (1–3 paragraphs) taken from the middle of a paper written by a fictitious student. The subject matter will be similar to that of the long papers in that it will be a research paper or personal essay. Entire sentences could be numbered, or words and/or phrases could be underlined and numbered

WRITING

for easy reference. Since you will only see a section of a paper, it is unlikely that you will be asked any questions about purpose or intent of the paper, but you will probably be asked about grammar.

> The sections of papers will not be sections of the long papers that you may see earlier in the test. They will be different passages on different topics.

LETTERS

These passages will be letters written by a fictitious student for some specific purpose, such as requesting a job or asking for information. Entire sentences could be numbered, or words and/or phrases may be underlined and numbered for easy reference. You may be asked about the purpose or intent of the letter, but you will probably be asked more questions about grammar or the arrangement of the letter.

STORIES

These passages could be from a few paragraphs to a page or two in length. They will be complete stories or excerpts from longer stories or books. They may be original works you have never seen before, or they may be sections of works with which you are already familiar. You will not be asked about the grammar in the story, but about the purpose or tone of the story or factual data (like the reading comprehension questions you usually see on tests about stories).

> Sometimes a story will only have a few multiple-choice questions following it. Other times, a story could be followed by several multiple-choice questions and may also be the prompt for an essay. If this is the case, be sure to reread at least the first part of the story before you start the writing process to make sure you're answering the question directly.

Other Documents

There are lots of other types of documents you could see on the writing test. In general, they will be there to support one of the types of passages we've already discussed.

Factual reports—You may be asked to read a factual report on the same topic as a story you've read for the test. The factual report will probably approach the topic from a different perspective. Your task on the questions will be to not only recognize the differences between the two passages, but also to be able to pick out thematic and structural similarities between them.

Notices—You may be asked to read notices as support materials for either letters or stories. These notices could be anything, ranging from help wanted ads from a newspaper, to advertisements, to graphs or charts. They add context to the other main materials you have read.

The Questions

The following are the types of questions you may be asked on your exit-level writing exam. You may see all of these types of questions, or only one or two, so be sure you are familiar with all of them.

READING COMPREHENSION

Reading comprehension questions are just like all the reading comprehension questions you've ever seen on any English test. They ask, directly or indirectly, about something that happened in the story. The best way to answer these questions is to go back to the passage and read the part to which the question refers. Then, answer the question in your own words by paraphrasing what you read in your mind. Once you've made your own paraphrase, go through the answer choices and eliminate any that don't match your answer to the question. If you are left with more than one answer choice, choose the one that is most like your answer.

Tone

Tone questions are usually asked about stories or other documents, not papers or letters written by students. These questions ask about the tone or effect that the author is trying to achieve. Use cues from the passage to eliminate the answer choices that aren't correct. For the most part, the writing test is not trying to trick you, so use common sense.

If the passage is personal in nature, like a memoir or a daughter's remembrance of her mother, for instance, the tone is not likely to be negative. It is also not likely to sound impersonal or ambivalent. Instead, it is most likely to be warm, loving, or nostalgic. Likewise, if the passage is a piece of nonfiction writing, it is unlikely to be extremely negative or positive. Good choices for a nonfiction passage would be words like *persuasive* or *informative.*

Remember that you are trying to eliminate the choices that aren't correct instead of just jumping at the choice that seems like it might be the answer. If you are really stuck, pick the answer choice that seems least extreme. In other words, pick the more moderate choice.

> Tone and purpose questions ask about the way the author writes and not about details within the passage. Don't get confused by any answer choices that refer to details from within the story.

Purpose

Purpose questions ask what the purpose or intent of the passage is. To answer this question correctly, reread the first paragraph and last paragraph (or first sentence and last sentence, if it's a short passage) as a kind of summary of the entire passage. Think about what the main message of the first paragraph and the last paragraph of the passage are. Write down a very brief (only a phrase or two) summary of the main message *before you even look at the answer choices.* Then, go through the answer choices and eliminate anything that doesn't sound at all similar to the summary you wrote down. If you still have more than one answer choice left, reread the first sentence of the whole passage again, and pick the answer choice that best expresses the purpose of the first sentence.

Grammar

Grammar questions ask about a specific underlined word or phrase or a numbered sentence. The specific item may or may not have something grammatically wrong with it.

One type of grammar question will ask you to choose a better way of expressing that item, and your task is to choose from one of the answer choices. The other type of grammar question will ask you to identify the underlined part and choose the best answer.

For the first type of question, skim through the answer choices to see if there is one indicating that "no changes are necessary." If there is, continue. If there isn't, skip to the next step. You should read the sentence in question and determine whether or not there really is a grammar error. (If you do not feel confident about your ability to determine if there's an error or not, go back and read Chapter 3 again.) If there isn't, choose the answer choice that says, "no changes are necessary," "as it is," or perhaps, "no correction is necessary" and go on to the next question.

If there is no answer choice indicating that "no changes are necessary," this means that there is definitely a grammar error in the sentence. Read the sentence and identify the error. Do not change the sentence or underlined part in your head. This will only cause more work for you in the long run, since it is likely that your exact change won't be one of the answer choices. Instead, figure out exactly what needs to be fixed to make the grammar correct. For example, you might note that the verb needs to be in present tense, or that the word should be an adverb, not an adjective. Jot this down quickly next to the question. Then, go through the answer choices and eliminate anything that doesn't perform the fix you wrote down. If you are left with more than one answer choice, pick the one that is the simplest. Let's try one:

Example: I have three years of experience teaching children <u>playing</u> softball during the summer.

Which of the following choices would fix the error in the sentence above?

(A) play

(B) to play

(C) played

(D) plays

There must be a grammar error in this sentence, since none of the answer choices say "no changes are necessary." The error is that you can't say, "teaching . . . playing." Instead you need a verb in its original form to follow *teaching*. *Play*, *played*, and *plays* have all been modified to tell what timeframe and who is doing the action. The only choice in the original form is "to play"; therefore, choice (B) is the correct answer.

Grammar questions may seem frightening, but if you have a good understanding of grammar you will do well on them. Don't forget to review Chapter 3 of this book if you are still having problems.

The other type of grammar question asks a straightforward question about the grammar in the sentence. We saw an example of this type of question in the section about process of elimination. In this example, the question asked what part of speech a word was. Your task is to identify the part of speech (go back to the chapter on grammar if you need to) and eliminate all the answer choices that can't be correct.

Revision

A revision question asks you to change something about a passage to improve it. You may be asked to change a word, phrase, or sentence; to add a sentence; or to delete a sentence. You may even be asked to change the order of several sentences.

Before you look at the answer choices, read the part of the passage to which the question refers. Try to decide what could be improved about the section. Does it need to be clearer? Is there a sentence that veers off-topic? Is something not explained adequately? Then, go through the answer choices and eliminate any that wouldn't make the change that you deemed necessary. If you are left with more than one answer choice, pick the one that makes the passage most clear.

Synonym

A synonym question will ask about a specific word in the passage. The question will provide several answer choice words. Your task is to pick the one that is closest in meaning to the underlined word in the passage. To do this, read the sentence containing the underlined word. Before you look at the answer choices, choose your own word to take the place of the underlined word in the sentence that will not change the sentence's meaning. Jot down this word next to the question. Then, go through the answer choices and eliminate every one that does NOT mean the same thing as the word you wrote down. Let's try it:

Example: Callas's strength was her <u>prodigious</u> vocal range of four full octaves.

Which of the following words is closest in meaning to the word *prodigious* in the sentence above?

(A) enormous

(B) limited

(C) varied

(D) ancient

CHAPTER 4

> If you don't know what the underlined word means, use clues from the rest of the sentence to help you figure it out. If you don't know what one of the answer choice words means, decide whether you should eliminate the others or not. If you've eliminated everything else, choose the word you don't know. If you still have another choice left, pick that one instead of the word you don't know.

Read the sentence and choose a word to replace *prodigious* that maintains the meaning of the sentence. The sentence talks about how big Callas's range was, so how about *large*? Now eliminate any answer choices that don't mean *large*. The only one left is *enormous*, so choice (A) must be the answer.

Other Question Types

You may encounter other types of questions on the multiple-choice section of the test. If you are asked a type of question you haven't seen before, just stay calm and follow the steps of process of elimination to answer it. Let's try one:

Example: Darnell has just received the assignment to write an autobiographical essay about an important moment in his life.

The first step Darnell will take to prepare to write this essay is most likely to be

(A) going to the library to begin researching the paper.

(B) asking his mother about her memories of her own childhood.

(C) writing down his strongest memories from his childhood.

(D) studying the grammar rules of *who* vs. *whom*.

MULTIPLE-CHOICE QUESTIONS

> If you see a question type you've never seen before, just stay calm and follow the directions given on the test. The process of elimination is the best way to work through any multiple-choice question, so stick with the system.

To answer this question, think logically about what you would do if you were Darnell. To start writing an essay about yourself, you'd probably start writing down things you remember. You certainly wouldn't do research at the library because the library wouldn't have any information about your own memories. It also wouldn't make sense to ask your mother what she remembers from her childhood, since the essay is about you. Lastly, the grammar rules of *who* vs. *whom* probably won't have anything to do with this essay. Therefore, the correct answer is (C).

CHAPTER 4

Pop Quiz

Directions: Questions 1–7 refer to the following paragraph. Read the paragraph, and then answer the questions that follow.

(1) Preparing for a party is all ways a hard thing to do. (2) If you clean your house a head of time, it makes it easier. (3) You have to plan because you do not want the party to be boaring. (4) I have been too many parties where I was bored. (5) A good party has got to have music and food. (6) If you make these selections in advance, you're guests are sure to have a good time. (7) If they have a good time, they'll probably come back, next year.

1. Sentence 1: Preparing for a party is all ways a hard thing to do.
   What correction should be made to this sentence?
   (A) change <u>is</u> to <u>as</u>
   (B) change <u>all ways</u> to <u>always</u>
   (C) put a semicolon after <u>party</u>
   (D) No corrections are necessary.

2. Sentence 2: If you clean your house a head of time, it makes it easier.
   What correction should be made to this sentence?
   (F) replace <u>your</u> with <u>you're</u>
   (G) change <u>a head</u> to <u>ahead</u>
   (H) replace <u>If</u> with <u>Since</u>
   (J) No corrections are necessary.

3. Sentence 3: You have to plan because you do not want the party to be boaring.
   What correction should be made to this sentence?
   (A) replace <u>because</u> with <u>since</u>
   (B) end the sentence with an exclamation mark
   (C) change <u>boaring</u> to <u>boring</u>
   (D) No corrections are necessary.

4. Sentence 4: I have been too many parties where I was bored.

   What correction should be made to this sentence?

   (F) change <u>too</u> to <u>to</u>

   (G) change <u>have</u> to <u>had</u>

   (H) replace <u>where</u> with <u>wear</u>

   (J) No corrections are necessary.

5. Sentence 5: A good party has got to have music and food.

   What correction should be made to this sentence?

   (A) insert <u>have</u> before <u>food</u>

   (B) change <u>has got to</u> to <u>must</u>

   (C) insert a colon after <u>have</u>

   (D) No corrections are necessary.

6. Sentence 6: If you make these selections in advance, you're guests are sure to have a good time.

   What correction should be made to this sentence?

   (F) replace <u>these</u> with <u>this</u>

   (G) change <u>you're</u> to <u>your</u>

   (H) replace <u>If</u> with <u>Where</u>

   (J) No corrections are necessary.

7. Sentence 7: If they have a good time, they'll probably come back, next year.

   What correction should be made to this sentence?

   (A) insert <u>the</u> before <u>next</u>

   (B) delete <u>probably</u>

   (C) delete the second comma

   (D) No corrections are necessary.

PT/HSPA, FCAT, MEAP HST, MCAS, GEE21, Regents Exams, SOL, NCCT, AHSGE, GHSGT,
NCCT, AHSGE, GHSGT, BST, BSAP, WASL, CAHSEE, TAAS, OGT, HSPT/HSPA, FCAT, MEA
GT, HSPT/HSPA, FCAT, MEAP HST, MCAS, GEE21, Regents Exams, SOL, NCCT, AHSGE, G
GHSGT, BST, BSAP, WASL, CAHSEE, TAAS, OGT, HSPT/HSPA, FCAT, MEAP HST, MCAS

CHAPTER
4

Answers and Explanations

1. **The correct answer is (B).** The correct word is <u>always</u> instead of the two words <u>all ways</u>.

2. **The correct answer is (G).** The two words <u>a head</u> should be replaced with <u>ahead</u>.

3. **The correct answer is (C).** The word <u>boring</u> is the correct word to use in this sentence.

4. **The correct answer is (F).** The word <u>too</u> should be replaced with its homonym <u>to</u>.

5. **The correct answer is (C).** The phrase <u>has got to</u> weakens the sentence.

6. **The correct answer is (G).** The contraction <u>you're</u> should be replaced with the possessive <u>your</u>.

7. **The correct answer is (C).** The second comma is not needed and should be deleted.

CHAPTER 5

WRITING

Now that you've refreshed your memory about the finer points of grammar, it's time to talk about writing essays on the writing test. While it's tempting to just skip this section and go in and wing it on test day, that would be a bad idea. Even if you're a great essay writer, you will write a better essay and the process will be much easier if you spend some time preparing before you go into the exam.

You might say, "But exactly how much can I really prepare? I won't know the essay topic until I start the test. And writing is so mysterious anyway—you can either do it or you can't." Wrong. Writing is a process, just as solving an algebra problem is a process. And the more you think of writing as a series of actions rather than a "magical journey," the better you'll do on the test.

Being born a super-genius at writing doesn't happen to many people. Instead, the majority of good writers become that way by establishing a system and sticking to it. You can learn to write well—or at least well enough to pass the writing test—by adapting our system to your own style and needs and then practicing it until it becomes second nature.

What the Test Graders Are Looking For

Before we embark on a discussion of our system, we should give some consideration to what the people who will be grading your essays want to see. For the most part, these readers are teachers or graduate students, not the people who actually wrote the test. This means that the readers are given a set of criteria to follow when grading the essays.

> Bear in mind that since everyone in your grade in the state takes the test at the same time, thousands of essays need to be graded in a short amount of time.

Thousands of essays graded by not so many readers means that the readers don't have time to do an in-depth critique of each essay, so they'll be even more reliant on the list of criteria to guide their grading.

In general, the readers who score your essays will be looking for (not necessarily in this order):

- ☑ Strong ideas
- ☑ Supportive examples and/or reasoning

HIGH STAKES

☑ Correct grammar

☑ Good organization. You should use distinct paragraphs, clearly delineated.

☑ Good length. Longer is better than shorter, although you shouldn't pad your essay just to make it fill up all the space.

☑ Fluid English. Your writing should flow smoothly, without awkward sentences or phrases.

☑ No errors or only minor errors. The readers won't take points off for one or two small misspellings or punctuation errors, but too many will hurt your score.

It's not a particularly tricky list of things to achieve, but, again, using a system helps. So let's get the show on the road.

Our System

Now that we've convinced you of the necessity of using a system, here it is.

Step 1. Assess the topic. What kind of essay are you writing?

Step 2. Brainstorm. Get it all out of your head and onto the paper.

Step 3. Organize. Rearrange everything into an outline that flows and makes sense.

Step 4. Write. Just do it.

Step 5. Revise. Read what you've written and make changes.

Step 6. Rewrite. Just do it again.

Step 7. Proofread. Make sure there are no spelling or grammar mistakes before you turn it in.

This system can be used to write anything, anywhere, at any time. We're going to show you specifically how it applies to the writing test in the rest of this chapter.

Step 1. Assess the Topic: What Type of Essay Are You Writing?

Writing an essay can cover a lot of topics, so you need to be sure you know what type of essay you should be writing. For instance, you don't want to write an essay attempting to persuade the graders that green is the best color if the directions actually ask you to describe how green would taste if green were a flavor instead of a color. It's important to know exactly what you need to accomplish with your writing. (This is good advice in general, not just about writing tests, by the way.)

> Don't just jump into brainstorming before you stop to think about how you should best answer the question. Look before you leap.

In this section we'll describe the main categories of essays that you'll see on writing tests and explain the subcategories, as well as how to attack them.

State and Support an Opinion

This type of essay asks you to state your opinion on a topic and then provide support for this opinion by using reasoning and/or examples. This is the type of essay that most people think of when they hear the words "essay test" (probably because this is the type of writing most often taught in middle and high school).

The steps to tackling this type of essay prompt are clear:

1. Make a decision.

2. State your opinion.

3. List the reasons you feel the way you do.

Pro/Con Essays

One subcategory of "state and support an opinion" essays is the essay type that asks you to choose one side of an argument. These are known as pro/con essays. The question itself is usually a statement, and you are asked to state your opinion either in favor of or against the statement and to explain your position. For instance, the essay question may be presented in the following way:

"The truth shall set you free." Do you agree or disagree with this statement? Why?

You first have to decide whether you think that the truth will, in fact, set you free, or that it won't set you free at all. Then, you write down your reasons for coming to that conclusion, and the essay practically writes itself.

What Would You Do?

Another subcategory of "state and support" essays asks you to make a decision and then provide support for your decision. The essay question may present you with a scenario and ask you to state what you would do if placed in that particular scenario and why you made that particular choice. For example:

Imagine that you have just won $2 million in a sweepstakes. What would you do with the money, and why?

Or, it may ask you to simply state a preference and then support it:

Do you prefer to eat at restaurants or at home most often? Why?

> Once you have stated your decision or position, the rest of the essay is simply a matter of supporting your opinion.

Sometimes this subcategory can take the form of a persuasive essay, which tends to be fairly formal:

The school board of Freeportsburg has just issued a press release stating that there will be a budget deficit in the school system of 10 percent for the

PT/HSPA, FCAT, MEAP HST, MCAS, GEE21, Regents Exams, SOL, NCCT, AHSGE, GHSGT, NCCT, AHSGE, GHSGT, BST, BSAP, WASL, CAHSEE, TAAS, OGT, HSPA, FCAT, MEA GT, HSPT/HSPA, FCAT, MEAP HST, MCAS, GEE21, Regents Exams, NCCT, AHSGE, G

CHAPTER
5

coming year. If you were in a position to solve this problem, what would you recommend the school board do and why?

Although the topic and language may be more substantial and formal than in an essay asking about your eating habits, your thought and writing process should be the same.

The Letter

Another subcategory of the "state and support" category is the letter. You may be asked to write a letter applying for a job, recommending some action to a committee or group, or persuading a group of readers to change their opinions. Although the format is different from that of a standard essay, your task is still to make a decision, state it, and then list reasons supporting your decision. For instance, in a letter applying for a job, your position is that the recipient of the letter should hire you (or at least give you an interview). To state this position you would write something like:

> ☑ *Please consider me for the position of . . .*

> ☑ *I'm writing to apply for the position of . . .*

Then, the rest of the letter would elaborate on the reasons why you are the perfect person for the job. If the letter is to recommend action, you would state the action you want the group to take (whether it is giving someone an award, installing a wheelchair ramp at your school, or something entirely different) and then state why they should take this action. A letter to the editor of a local or school paper is written in an attempt to get a group of readers to change their opinions on a topic. It follows the same format: state your opinion and then the reasons it makes sense.

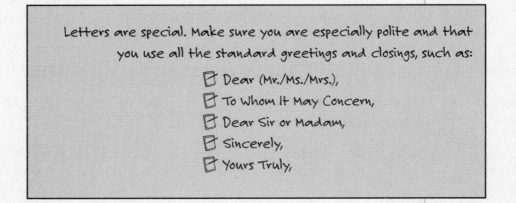

Letters are special. Make sure you are especially polite and that you use all the standard greetings and closings, such as:

☑ Dear (Mr./Ms./Mrs.),
☑ To Whom It May Concern,
☑ Dear Sir or Madam,
☑ Sincerely,
☑ Yours Truly,

HIGH STAKES

SHOW ADVANTAGES AND DISADVANTAGES

The third category of essay asks you to explore both sides of an issue by explaining the advantages and disadvantages of a given course of action. For example, the essay prompt may say:

Some people have suggested that the song "God Bless America" should replace "The Star Spangled Banner" as the national anthem of the United States. Explore the advantages and disadvantages of this plan.

This essay has many similarities to the essay asking you to choose a side and support it, except that once you've chosen one side and supported it with reasoning and examples, you have to support the other side of the argument in the same essay.

The most difficult aspect of this type of essay is organization. You can show all the advantages of one side and then all the disadvantages, almost as if you've written two essays and just tacked the second one onto the first. Or you can show an advantage followed by a disadvantage, alternating throughout the essay. How you choose to organize the essay is up to you, but you should think about it now and decide how you'll organize an essay like this if you are given one on your test. That way you'll have one less thing to think about while you take your exam.

EXPLAIN WHY

This type of essay asks you to explain a process or structure or to explain why something happens. It may ask about something

- **historical** (like why the stock market crashed in 1929);

- **sociological** (like why certain books are more popular with high school students today than they were with high school students in the 1950s); or

- **literary** (like explaining the motivation or action in a given passage).

This type of essay doesn't ask for much creativity in terms of reasoning or examples. Instead, it asks for logic, organization, and detail.

Once you've identified the type of essay you'll be writing, move on to the next step—brainstorming.

PT/HSPA, FCAT, MEAP HST, MCAS, GEE21, Regents Exams, SOL, NCCT, AHSGE, GHSGT, NCCT, AHSGE, GHSGT, BST, BSAP, WASL, CAHSEE, TAAS, OGT, HSPA, FCAT, MEA GT, HSPT/HSPA, FCAT, MEAP HST, MCAS, GEE21, Regents Exams, NCCT, AHSGE, G GHSGT, BST, BSAP, WASL, CAHSEE, TAAS, OGT, HSPT/HSPA, FCAT, MEAP HST, MCAS

CHAPTER
5

Step 2. Brainstorm

While theoretically it is possible to read the essay question, take out your pen, and start writing the essay, there's a better way. It's called brainstorming, and it allows you to dump everything you've got in your head that even vaguely relates to the topic out on paper. Then, later on you can sort through your ideas to see which ones you want to keep and which ones you can ignore. Think of it this way: If you've got a big bag full of junk, and you're trying to find one specific object, how can you find that object most efficiently? It wouldn't be smart to keep sticking your hand in the bag, feeling around to try to find that one specific thing amidst everything else in the bag. The most direct way would be to dump everything out of the bag and spread it out so you can see what you've got. The thing you're looking for should be easy to spot, and then you can just stuff everything else back in the bag.

Use the same idea to write an essay. If you just start writing and try to come up with and remember ideas while at the same time organizing, choosing the right words, and keeping track of your spelling, you'll be expending more energy than you need to. It's much more direct to write down all your ideas. Then you can organize them as a separate step, and then write the essay later.

Before you can begin writing everything down, though, the first thing you should do when you read the essay question is decide what your main point is going to be. Some essays require that you pick a side of an argument or explain your opinion on something. Others require that you enumerate both sides of an issue. Still others require that you describe a process. The type of question determines the way you can brainstorm. If you've completed the first step of the process by assessing the question, you've already determined what type of essay you'll be writing. If not, go back and review the first part of this chapter.

You can't even begin the process without a clear understanding of the question. Practice on the exercises at the end of this book. If you still have problems understanding what they're asking, you should ask your English teacher for help before the day of the test.

If you're writing an essay in which you debate a topic or support your opinion, you need to pick a side. Write down a phrase expressing that thought, like "welfare reform is bad" or "why I want to be an astronaut." Then, write down all the ideas that come into your head. You can either write them straight down the side of the page or make a mind map. To make a mind map, write the main idea in the center of the page and circle it. Then write each new idea, as you think of it, as a ray radiating from the center idea. As you think of supporting ideas or examples, link them to the things you've already written down. This provides a more visual, less linear method of writing down your ideas.

Just for kicks, let's try it now. Try brainstorming the old fashioned way (by making a list). Use this topic:

If someone gave you $500, what would you do with the money and why?

1.

2.

3.

Now, try brainstorming by making a mind map for the following topic:

In your opinion, who was the most important person of the twentieth century and why?

We've started the structure of the mind map for you. Please feel free to add new branches and bubbles as your ideas form.

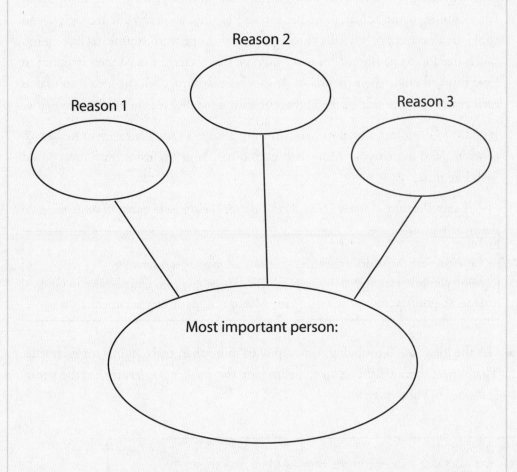

With which method did you feel most comfortable? Try using that method whenever you need to make a list or to brainstorm between now and the day of the test. There are more questions on which to practice your brainstorming skills at the end of this book.

If you're debating an issue (such as whether or not the truth will set you free), you need to come up with several examples or reasons to support your point. You may, however, also want to think of some reasoning that could be used to argue the opposite of your opinion. If you can state these examples and then prove that they aren't true or don't matter, you'll strengthen your essay.

HIGH STAKES

The question may, however, ask you to state both sides of an issue without picking a side. In this case, you need to come up with several good reasons for each side. A good way to do this is to write down the flip side of each point you come up with. For example, if the topic is reasons for and against a curfew for teenagers, you could say that teenagers need a curfew so they don't get into trouble by having too much freedom. The flip side of this would be that teenagers need their freedom to have fun and enjoy their friends while they're still young. So, the idea is to match each reason on one side of the argument with a parallel reason on the other side.

It's hard to use a mind map to brainstorm this way. It's usually easier to make two columns, and match your ideas with each other. Your brainstorming sheet could look like this:

Essay Prompt: *Should "God Bless America" be the new national anthem?*

Yes	No
Easier to sing than current anthem	Not as impressive-sounding
More patriotic message	Offends people who don't believe in God
Doesn't glorify war	Message not as strong as current anthem

Get the idea? You'll probably come up with more than three points for each side. That's great, because then you can eliminate the weaker points and use the strongest ones in your essay.

> Do you have a better way of brainstorming that you're really comfortable using? As long as it doesn't involve making noise or jumping around on your desk, feel free to use it during the test.

If you're asked to describe a process or structure, try to write everything down in the order in which it occurs. If you forget something, use an arrow to indicate where it should go in the process. Mind maps don't always work to brainstorm this type of essay.

When you've written down everything you can think of, read the question again. Did you write down things that responded to the actual question? If not, start again. Did you think of anything else? If so, write it down. If not, move on to the next step—organizing.

Step 3. Organize

Look at your brainstorming notes. Pick out the three or four strongest ideas that best support your point. Put them in order from most impressive/strongest to least impressive/weakest. Write down any supporting examples or reasoning beneath each point.

You may not have to change anything from your original brainstorming notes. Once you've practiced the brainstorming and essay-writing process, your brainstorming will probably become more organized all by itself. Don't worry if you have to untangle a mess of thoughts, though. Better to do it now than to be stuck writing in the middle of the essay at a dead end.

Read the question again and look at your outline. Ask yourself:

- ☑ Does it make sense?

- ☑ Does it make your point?

- ☑ Does it directly answer the question? If not, change things until it really says what you want it to say.

> Organizing can be the most vital step of the entire process. If you organize well and make a great outline, the writing will be much easier and better than it will if you skimp on the organization.

HIGH STAKES

Organizing a "State and Support an Opinion" Essay

For a "state and support an opinion" essay, the organization is very straightforward. You should have an introduction, then 2 to 4 paragraphs, each including a reason for your opinion, with supporting examples for each reason. Don't forget a conclusion paragraph at the end.

Organizing an "Advantage/Disadvantage" Essay

For an "advantage/disadvantage" essay, you can organize the essay in two different ways. Let's use the anthem prompt as an example:

> Some people have suggested that the song "God Bless America" should replace "The Star Spangled Banner" as the national anthem of the United States. Explore the advantages and disadvantages of this plan.

One way to approach this essay is to list all the advantages, then all the disadvantages, like this:

Paragraph 1:   Introductory paragraph addressing the topic

Paragraph 2:
Advantages: Easier to sing than current anthem
                 More patriotic message
                 Doesn't glorify war

Paragraph 3:
Disadvantages: Not as impressive-sounding
                    Offends people who don't believe in God
                    Message not as strong as current anthem

Paragraph 4:   Conclusion

Another way to approaching this essay is to alternate advantages and disadvantages all the way through, like this:

Paragraph 1:   Introductory paragraph addressing the topic

Paragraph 2:   Easier to sing than current anthem

Not as impressive-sounding

Paragraph 3:   More patriotic message

Offends people who don't believe in God

Paragraph 4:   Doesn't glorify war

Message not as strong as current anthem

Paragraph 5:   Conclusion

> Organizing an essay describing a process or structure is easy; just go in chronological or spatial order.

When you brainstormed you probably got pretty close to the actual organization you'll use to write your paper. If not, use arrows to insert any missing or misplaced thoughts. When you are finished organizing your thoughts, you're ready to write!

Step 4. Write

This step is the one that most people fear. But if you've gone through the steps of brainstorming and organizing an outline, the writing is almost an afterthought. All you really have to do is make paragraphs out of your outline and connect them in a fluid and logical manner. Those of you who have a hard time believing it's that easy should read the rest of this section to learn how to write the paragraphs and put them together.

HIGH STAKES

PARAGRAPHS

Every paragraph needs a topic sentence that tells what the entire paragraph is about. While in a piece of fiction the topic sentence can be anywhere within the paragraph, for your writing test you should always place the topic sentence at the beginning of the paragraph. Since the topic sentence is the first thing in each paragraph that the grader will read, it needs to be direct and clear but also have punch.

Make sure you know what the main point of the paragraph should be, then write it down. If you are having problems with the flow of the words, think about how you would explain the point of the paragraph to your best friend. Write it down that way, but without using slang. While language that is too simple can sound too informal, overly complicated language and structure makes you appear to be trying too hard and you risk using words you don't fully understand.

> It's better to stick with clear, concise language that you understand than to risk using a word incorrectly.

For example, if the point of the paragraph is "If you tell the truth, you don't have to feel guilty," the following topic sentence would be too convoluted:

> *When confronted with the question of whether or not to tell the truth, as we are, it bears mentioning that freedom from deception means freedom from immorality.*

A better topic sentence would be:

> *Telling the truth can be freeing because it eliminates the need for feelings of guilt.*

It's not as fancy, but it's easier to read and understand, and it gets the point across. It also sets up the rest of the paragraph.

Once you have a great topic sentence, you should use the rest of the paragraph to make your argument. The best way to shore up your argument is to provide the evidence and reasoning you wrote down when you brainstormed. Present it in a clear, direct way. Do not use sensational language (like exaggerated claims or exclamations) or rhetorical questions. Instead, be direct and build your argument a step at a time.

> If you're having problems, write your topic sentence last. Since you'll be revising and rewriting the whole essay, wait until you have almost everything else written, then base your topic sentence on what you've already done.

Use Concrete Details

One common mistake students make when writing essays is to make broad claims and then neglect to back them up with details. The broad claims may sound impressive, but the whole paragraph falls apart when there are no concrete supporting examples or reasoning. This means that you need to make an extra effort to flesh out your point with solid details. For example, instead of saying:

> *Everyone knows what happened to the Roman Empire. Therefore, we should eliminate violence in movies.*

you should say something more detailed, such as:

> *Violence in movies should be eliminated because it will eventually cause the end of our society. History has provided us with examples of societies that were ruined because of a decline in values. One example is the Roman Empire, which fell because of violence. The wars and backstabbing that ultimately killed the Empire were the inevitable conclusion of the immoral behavior of the Romans over hundreds of years. There is no reason to think that what happened to the Romans won't happen to us in the long run, if we continue to allow anything and everything to be broadcast publicly.*

As you can see, adding concrete details proves the point, while withholding details makes the paragraph sound ridiculous and weak.

Write in Order of Importance

Just as the entire essay becomes more powerful when you organize it so that the most important points come first, any given paragraph is most effective when you start off with the most important ideas. We've already covered the importance of starting each paragraph with a topic sentence so the reader knows what the point of the paragraph will be. The next sentence should introduce the reasoning behind the topic sentence. The following sentences should each support and provide more information on the sentence before it. The last sentence of the paragraph should complete the connection between the topic sentence and the reasoning behind it.

One way to think of this structure is as an upside-down V. You start with a general principle in the topic sentence. The next sentence is more specific, and each proceeding sentence gets more and more specific. If you violate this rule, the paragraph won't make much sense. Take a look at what the paragraph about violence in movies would say if we rearranged the sentences, even slightly, so they weren't in the upside-down V order:

> *Violence in movies should be eliminated because it will eventually cause the end of our society. One example is the Roman Empire, which fell because of violence. The wars and backstabbing that ultimately killed the Empire were the inevitable conclusion of the immoral behavior of the Romans over hundreds of years. History has provided us with examples of societies that were ruined because of a decline in values. There is no reason to think that what happened to the Romans won't happen to us in the long run, if we continue to allow anything and everything to be broadcast publicly.*

It still kind of makes sense, but it just doesn't have that same power to lure you into the argument and really convince you of the author's point.

CHAPTER 5

Have you heard the saying, "Location is everything"? Well, it applies in essay writing, too. Putting your points or sentences in the wrong order can weaken an otherwise well-done essay.

Unity and Coherence

One sure way to ruin a good paragraph is to insert a sentence that goes off topic. While you may be tempted to add some random detail that you know just to pad the paragraph, it will ultimately hurt you more than a shorter paragraph would. Each paragraph needs to flow; every sentence should be contributing directly to making your point. If it doesn't, then you should rethink the sentence. Either change the sentence to apply to the point of the paragraph, or eliminate it entirely. Notice how adding just one off-topic sentence weakens the whole paragraph:

Violence in movies should be eliminated because it will eventually cause the end of our society. History has provided us with examples of societies that were ruined because of a decline in values. One example is the Roman Empire, which fell because of violence. The wars and backstabbing that ultimately killed the Empire were the inevitable conclusion of the immoral behavior of the Romans over hundreds of years. The Roman Empire officially fell in 476 C.E. when Odoacer the Scirian deposed Romulus Augustus. There is no reason to think that what happened to the Romans won't happen to us in the long run, if we continue to allow anything and everything to be broadcast publicly.

The whole paragraph is contributing to the idea that violence in a society can lead to its end, but the argument is interrupted with the out-of-place information about Odoacer the Scirian.

One off-topic sentence brings the whole argument to a screeching halt.

The last sentence of the paragraph, which really ties the whole argument together, loses its effectiveness by following the sentence about Odoacer the Scirian.

All Together Now

To sum up what we've talked about so far:

- Start with the topic sentence
- Use details
- Put things in the upside-down V order of importance
- Stay on topic

Let's take a look at what happens when you don't do these things versus when you do. The following is a bad paragraph:

When confronted with the question of whether or not to tell the truth, as we are, it bears mentioning that freedom from deception means freedom from immorality. After all, who among us hasn't felt the stomachache of guilt at a lie or half-truth? And we all should, because lying is wrong. But that doesn't help the person who is caught in a web of deceit. Emotional freedom is as important as physical freedom is.

Let's analyze why this paragraph is bad. First, the topic sentence is confusing and uses language that the author doesn't really seem to understand. The whole thing is vague, and the sentence that should follow the topic sentence is at the end of the paragraph. The paragraph about lying being wrong is off-topic. Lastly, the author uses a rhetorical question and a cliché that would sound better on the back of a paperback novel ("web of deceit"). The next paragraph is far better:

Telling the truth can be freeing because it eliminates the need for feelings of guilt. If you tell the truth, you have nothing to hide, and therefore a clear conscience. Although confessing the truth can be painful in the short run, it provides a long-term payoff by freeing you from anxiety and worry. This, in turn, leaves you free to think about other things that will benefit you and others.

This paragraph starts with a clear topic sentence and is followed by a direct explanation of the topic sentence. The third sentence supports the second one, and the last sentence ties the argument together. The author explains the reasoning in detail and doesn't include anything off-topic. It is a strong paragraph that helps convince the reader that the author has a valid opinion, which is the goal of any essay.

More on Paragraphs

Paragraph Accuracy

You can write a paragraph using the ideas in the previous section and still have a weak-sounding essay if you aren't careful to use verb tenses, time relationships, and point of view properly.

> These things seem small in comparison to the major issues we covered earlier. But, they can seriously affect your score if you do them incorrectly.

Use Correct Verb Tenses—"Use correct verb tenses" seems like the kind of tip that you'd get from someone who was just trying to bug you. But it's one of the things that students tend to be most casual about when writing for tests. Since you only have a short time and this one writing sample to prove your proficiency at writing to graders who don't know you personally, it's extra important to be precise about the verb tenses you choose. Think about the purpose of each sentence you write, and choose a tense accordingly. Look at this sentence:

History has taught us a lesson if we only listen to it.

The sentiment of the sentence is good, but it doesn't actually make any sense, since the author used a past tense ("has taught") instead of a present tense ("can teach").

The appropriate use of each of the verb tenses is covered in Chapter 3 of this book, so we won't repeat all that information here. If you skimmed it the first time, go back and read it more carefully now.

Use Simple Tenses—The verb tenses you use in a writing test essay should be simple, not complicated. Since all you will be doing is explaining, giving examples, and reasoning, you won't need to use complex time relationships or tenses to make your argument.

If you find yourself using unnecessarily complex verb tenses, rethink your sentence to see if you can make it more direct.

For an example, take a look at this sentence:

The Roman Empire's decline would not have had to occur if it would not have been for the excessive violence with which the entire society had been living for centuries.

The sentence could be made less confusing and complex by changing it to:

Because the society of the Roman Empire had lived with excessive violence for centuries, the Empire ultimately declined.

Show Time Relationships—Try to remember that the reader of your essay does not have any prior knowledge of the things you write about, so you should use words showing time relationships very carefully. Don't switch tenses or use time markers unnecessarily. For example, look at the following paragraph:

I'm walking down the street, minding my own business, when all of a sudden I get hit on the arm by a blob of paint. Startled, I looked up to see where the paint had come from.

Do you see the problem with those sentences? The first one is written in present tense ("I'm *walking* ... *minding* ... I *get hit* ..."), but the second one switches to past tense ("I *looked* ... paint *had come* ...") for no reason. It's pretty common for people to do this when they tell stories to their friends, but it's not proper writing, and it can weaken an otherwise good essay.

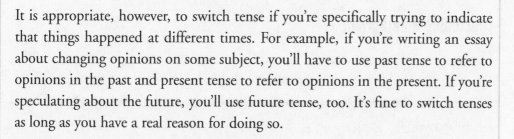

> Beware of casual speech on the writing test. This extends to words that may not be written the way they sound. For example, many of us incorrectly pronounce the words "would have" as "would of" in the sentence, "I would have ordered the snails if I had known they were on the menu."

It is appropriate, however, to switch tense if you're specifically trying to indicate that things happened at different times. For example, if you're writing an essay about changing opinions on some subject, you'll have to use past tense to refer to opinions in the past and present tense to refer to opinions in the present. If you're speculating about the future, you'll use future tense, too. It's fine to switch tenses as long as you have a real reason for doing so.

Use a Consistent Point of View—Decide before you start writing which point of view you will use, and stick with it. You have several choices. You can write from the first-person perspective, using the word *I* frequently. This is appropriate especially if the wording of the question says something like "in your opinion" or "what would you do," or in cases where the topic is personal, such as an essay about your family or school.

You can also write from a third-person point of view and refer to everything as *it, he,* or *she.* Less commonly, you can use a second-person point of view (as we are here, referring to the reader as *you*) or use the word *one* to refer to any person. Using *one* is probably not the best choice, since it can lead to confusing and awkward sentences, like:

> *One should always remember that one's first instinct can save one from making a mistake and putting one's own life in danger.*

Ugly, huh? You'll be better off just staying away from *one* and using a less formal choice.

No matter what point of view you choose, you need to stick with that same one throughout your essay.

It will really confuse the reader if you've been using the third person and then all of a sudden switch into the second person. Consistency is key.

Concluding a Paragraph

Just as every paragraph needs a strong beginning, it also needs a strong finish. Don't lose steam because you're getting to the end—just push on through. We've talked a little about concluding a paragraph already, but let's discuss a few different ways to do it.

Methods of Concluding—In the previous section we said, "The last sentence of the paragraph should complete the connection between the topic sentence and the reasoning behind it." This is the most popular way to write a conclusion sentence, but it is not the only way. Other methods of concluding a paragraph are to transition or lead into the next paragraph, or to sum up the information in the entire paragraph.

Which method you choose depends on what you've already written and on what your purpose is in the essay. For instance, if you've written a long paragraph in which you explained a point very thoroughly, you may need to tie your topic sentence together with the end of the explanation so it all makes sense. On the other hand, if you're trying to make one big argument throughout the essay by building from point to point, it would be better to lead into the next paragraph to tie the paragraphs together.

Checklist for Writing Powerful Paragraphs

Use the following checklist to help you write powerful paragraphs:

- ☑ Start with a strong topic sentence.

- ☑ Follow this with the reasoning behind the point in the topic sentence.

- ☑ Build each successive sentence on the sentence before it, adding more detail and explanation.

- ☑ Use detail and stay on topic.

- ☑ Use correct, simple, and consistent verb tenses and point of view.

- ☑ Write an appropriate and direct conclusion sentence.

Turning Paragraphs into Essays

Now that you have great paragraphs written, you need to be able to string them together into a great essay. It's not so hard, as long as you can write a good introduction paragraph to present your point to the readers, connect your middle paragraphs with appropriate transition words, and sum it all up appropriately with a conclusion paragraph.

Writing an Introduction

Every essay needs an introductory paragraph. The function of an intro paragraph is simple: to introduce the issue and state what the essay will say about that issue.

This lets the reader know that you understood the question, have a clear opinion on the issue, and will be explaining your views in the essay. The topic sentence of the intro paragraph is the first impression the grader gets of your writing ability, so it should be the best sentence of the entire essay.

> Do not make the mistake of thinking that irony is your friend in the writing test format. Be as direct and clear as possible. Remember the time constraints on the readers, and don't make them do any more work to "crack" your essay than they have to.

HIGH STAKES

To introduce the issue, you should paraphrase the question in some way. Do not repeat the question word for word. This looks amateurish and makes the reader think you won't be making a good argument. Instead, summarize so that you can lead into the next part of the intro paragraph—what the essay will say about the issue. Of course it is technically possible to write an intro paragraph without ever committing to the position the essay will take, but this won't help your test score. A hallmark of good writing is the ability to communicate your ideas to the reader, so if the reader doesn't know what you think about the question by the end of the intro paragraph, your essay isn't well-written.

You may also want to give some background information on the topic in the intro paragraph, or use it to explore the other side of the argument without giving the opposition any support. The last sentence of the intro paragraph should lead the reader into the first point, which will follow immediately in the topic sentence of the second paragraph.

Using Good Transitions

You can write an essay with great insights and examples, but if it isn't well-organized, it won't score well on the test. This means that you should place as much emphasis on good organization of your essay as on any other single aspect.

One way to help maintain organization and make your structure obvious to the reader is to use transition words. You may recall transition words from the essays you wrote in sixth grade. Some of the most popular ones are:

First, second, third...last
Firstly, secondly, thirdly...lastly
Finally
Consequently
Conversely
Because of
As a result of

Moreover

Meanwhile

However

On the other hand

Then

Next

Furthermore

In conclusion

To sum up

There are tons more transition words, so feel free to use any you don't see on this list. The key is to use them to help the reader see the superior organization of your paper. You can take a minimalist approach by using the words *first, second, last,* and *in conclusion* to begin your third through fifth paragraphs, respectively. Or, you can really tailor your transition words to your argument. For instance, if your first two points support your idea, but the third point explores the opposing point of view, you might start that paragraph with the transition word *conversely*. You should use the exercises at the end of this book to practice using transition words so that you'll be comfortable with them on test day.

Writing a Conclusion

> The conclusion paragraph is almost as important as the intro paragraph, because it is the last thing the reader sees, and therefore the thing the reader remembers most.

While you don't have to introduce any new information in the conclusion paragraph, you do need to make sense, reinforce your argument, and make the whole essay sound finished.

A good structure for a conclusion paragraph is to start the first sentence with a transition word (of course) and then write a fairly general comment on the topic. The next sentence should make the claim that you have shown that your

WRITING

argument is valid. Summarize your points briefly in the next sentence or two, and finish by reiterating your argument. This paragraph could look like this:

> *In conclusion, the idea that the truth can set you free is both interesting and complex. In the previous essay, I have demonstrated that truth and freedom are related to each other. I have shown that freedom doesn't necessarily have anything to do with physical boundaries and that telling the truth frees a person from feelings of guilt and shame. In addition, I have proven that any so-called freedom that does not include truth and honesty is not really freedom at all. This all proves that the statement "the truth shall set you free" is valid.*

This is only one possible structure for a conclusion paragraph. We'll cover a few more in the sections about writing specific types of essays, but you can probably come up with one or two good ways to conclude all by yourself. Try them out on the exercises at the end of this book.

> Did we mention there are exercises at the end of the book? You're not done studying until you've worked through all of them, so sharpen your pencils.

Writing Specific Types of Essays

Writing an Essay Stating and Supporting an Opinion

The easiest way to begin your intro paragraph is to paraphrase the question. If the question says, *"The truth shall set you free." Do you agree or disagree with this statement? Why?*, you should change the words to indicate that there is debate on the topic. For example, you might write:

> *While some people feel that the truth will set them free, others do not agree with this idea.*

This sentence serves two purposes: it lets the reader know what the essay will be about, and it sets up the idea that there are two sides to the issue. You'll have to follow this sentence with one giving a little more information on the topic, though.

You might say:

The idea that truth and freedom may be connected is a complex one that needs to be considered carefully.

Or you could do the same thing in two sentences, but in a different way, like this:

Some people think that the truth will set them free because freedom comes from not keeping secrets. Others, however, would argue that truth and freedom are not connected at all.

Whichever way you choose to introduce the topic, your next sentence should state which side of the argument you're on. It may seem too predictable, but there's nothing wrong with following old standards: "In the following essay I will show that . . ." or "The following essay will prove that . . . ." Then, briefly list the points you will be making in the essay.

> If you're thinking that this all sounds so standardized, you're right. The point of this test is not to see what a great creative writer you are, but to see if you can write a standard essay or letter according to the conventions of American writing.

Use the same format if you are writing an essay about your opinion, but bear in mind that you won't be able to set up a pro/con situation in the first two sentences. Instead, you'll have to set up a "my opinion" vs. "the way others might think/do" situation. Here's an example:

Some people who win money in sweepstakes or the lottery invest the money. However, if I won $2 million, I would give it to my family and friends. In the following essay, I will explain why I would give away the money instead of keeping it. I will explain that I have strong family ties, that my parents deserve a financial reward for all they've been through, and that what you give ultimately comes back to you.

If you're writing a letter, some things will change. First, obviously you will need to write the date, your return address, the address of the recipient, and "Dear So-and-so." In the first sentence of the body of the letter you should state directly what you want, whether it's a job, an extended curfew time, or more candy bars in the school cafeteria. Then, use a few sentences to briefly explain the points you will be making in the rest of the letter.

WRITING

No matter what type of essay you're writing, the middle 2–4 paragraphs will stay the same: list your points, one in each paragraph, and follow with examples or reasoning to support them. Then, follow with a conclusion paragraph. In it, you should restate the main premise of the essay to bring it all full circle. Then, in a few sentences, summarize how you've proven your point.

A strong way to finish your essay is to use the conclusion paragraph to debunk the opposing argument.

The first sentence of the conclusion should, again, start with a transition word or phrase, but should then state the opposing point of view. The next sentence should support that view. The third and fourth sentences should challenge that view and provide more support for your own view. Use the final sentence of the paragraph to make the claim that your own view is valid. Here's an example:

Conversely, opponents of the idea that the truth can set you free claim that truth and freedom are not related at all. They say that a person can be physically free without being an honest person. However, I would respond that physical freedom alone isn't the point of the statement. True freedom is both physical and mental, and the only freedom worth having is mental freedom, which you can only have by being honest. To sum up, the statement "the truth shall set you free" is correct.

Writing an Essay Showing Advantages and Disadvantages

You can start an "advantage/disadvantage" essay the same way you start a "state and support" essay. Paraphrase the question, and then summarize the two different sides of the issue. The real difference is that instead of stating that you will show that one side is more valid than the other side is, you should state that you will explore both sides of the issue in the essay. An example of the wording for this is:

In the following essay, I will explore reasons that "God Bless America" should become our new national anthem as well as reasons that "The Star Spangled Banner" should remain the anthem.

We've already discussed the two different ways you can choose to present your points: either with all the advantages followed by all the disadvantages or with advantages and disadvantages alternating all the way through. Whichever way you organize your essay, be sure to use appropriate transition words. It is especially important to have a very obvious structure in an essay that can be confusing because the two sides are being argued simultaneously.

> Remember that the readers don't have a lot of time to spend untangling a complicated essay. Make it as easy for them as possible to give you a perfect score by making your structure obvious.

The conclusion paragraph should make a general statement about the topic. Then, you should sum up the two arguments in a manner parallel to the way you organized the essay.

Writing an Essay Explaining "Why"

An essay explaining "why" is completely different from the other two essay types. Since you're not really arguing a point, but simply chronicling and analyzing something, your language will be less persuasive. The first sentence of your intro paragraph should be a statement about the topic you're covering. Then, explain briefly what the issues involved are. The final sentence of the introductory paragraph should state the purpose of your essay.

The middle paragraphs should follow the outline you made in the organizing step of the process. Be sure to use appropriate transition words to show how things happened. You'll probably use words like *consequently, meanwhile,* and *in response to* more than you will the standard paragraph markers like *first, second,* and *last.* Your conclusion paragraph should be a brief summary of your essay, ending with another general statement about the topic.

WRITING

Step 5. Revise

Now that you have a first draft written, you could call it quits and just turn in what you have.

It's the revision step that truly separates the champs from the chumps, though.

Of course it's tempting just to turn it in and be done with the whole project, but you'll create a much better final product if you take the time to revise and write another draft.

Another real benefit to revising a paper and rewriting it is that you learn more about how you write and your own weaknesses. Eventually this will make the whole writing process easier for you. And that's a skill that will help you not only on the writing test, but also in college and whatever career you eventually have.

There are two levels that you need to look at. On a basic level, you need to make sure that everything you wrote is grammatically correct. On a more advanced level, you have to assess the structure and content of your essay. Structure and content errors are more difficult to spot and to fix, so start with those first.

When you're writing something in the real world (not on the exit-level writing test), the two best ways to revise a paper are to

- forget about it for a day or two so you can read it with fresh eyes, and

- ask a friend or family member to read it and give you feedback.

Unfortunately, there's really no way you can do either of these things on a timed writing test. Instead, you'll have to be your own friend and critique your paper honestly. The following list of questions should help you get started:

- Did I answer the question directly?

- Did I stick to the point throughout the paper, without going off on tangents?

- Can you tell from the first paragraph what the point of the paper is?

☑ Is my argument easy to follow, or is the paper vague or confusing in parts?

☑ Have I made any major grammatical mistakes?

☑ Did I use slang or other non-standard English?

☑ Did I back up any points I made with evidence or reasoning?

☑ Did I avoid redundancy and padding?

☑ Did I write a conclusion paragraph that makes a strong finish?

> These questions can help you any time you have to write an essay. Once you're done with the writing test, you might want to rip this page out of the book and tack it up on the wall where you write papers for school as a reference.

Read your paper with a critical eye and honestly assess its strengths and weaknesses in light of these questions. If you know you have other problems with your writing, look for those, too. Now that you've corrected the structure and content problems with your draft, hunting down the grammar errors should be relatively easy. Here's a list of grammar errors to look for:

☑ Sentences without subjects or verbs

☑ Sentences with mismatched subjects and verbs

☑ Incorrect pronouns

☑ Verb tense errors

☑ Misplaced modifiers (words or phrases)

☑ Mismatched comparisons or lists of things

☑ Sentences that are too long and complicated

☑ Sentences that are too simple

☑ Too many sentences that sound alike

☑ Language that is too casual or simple, or overly difficult

Make the corrections you need to, and write the revisions on the paper so you don't forget them. Then, move on to the next step—rewriting.

Step 6. Rewrite

If you made only minor revisions in the previous step, rewriting this draft will mostly be an exercise in copying to get a clean draft. If you made more extensive changes, though, this step can be really challenging. You may have to change or eliminate entire sentences and write new ones, or change things around.

> Don't be afraid to make big changes!

This is your last chance to say what you really want to say and score well on the test. Your hand may be cramped from writing, but you have to push on.

While it may seem obvious, it's worth saying that you should be careful not to make any new errors in this step. Just when you thought you were finally done with the whole mess and could turn it in, it's time to do the final step—proofreading.

Step 7. Proofread

While it may seem like a real pain to have to read through the essay again, you'll be extremely upset if you score poorly because of grammatical mistakes or slips of the pen. After all the work you've done assessing the question, brainstorming, organizing, writing, revising, and rewriting, it would be a shame to blow it all just because you were too tired to give it one last check for errors. You really owe it to yourself to do a final proofreading pass.

> Proofreading can be really painful. You're so close to being done that you can taste it, and going through your essay one last time is the *last* thing you want to do. Don't drop the ball before you cross the finish line, though, by skipping this important step.

The following items are common errors that you should check for:

☑ Misspelled words

☑ Words that aren't misspelled but aren't the words you want to use (such as *you* instead of *your*, *it's* instead of *its*, or any wrong use of *there, they're,* and *their*)

☑ Incorrect punctuation, especially commas, semicolons, colons, and dashes

☑ Run-on sentences

☑ Written "tics," such as starting too many sentences with words such as *so* or *then*

Fix any errors you find, then hand in your paper. You're done! Don't make your fellow test takers feel bad by gloating.

Pop Quiz

Directions: List the seven steps to writing essays. Check your answers in the chapter.

1.

2.

3.

4.

5.

6.

7.

Now, you're ready for the next chapter.

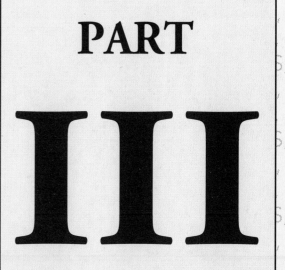

PART

III

EXERCISES

CHAPTER 6

WARM-UP AND MULTIPLE-CHOICE EXERCISES

This chapter is divided into two sections. The first is called "Warm-Up." Do these before you move on to the second section, "Multiple-Choice Exercises." There are answer keys and explanations at the end of this chapter.

Warm-Up Exercises

Exercise 1

Directions: The underlined word or phrase may or may not be correct grammatically. Choose the correct answer from the four choices.

1. Yesterday the humidity level downtown <u>is reaching</u> 70 percent, but today it is only expected to reach 40 percent.

    (A) No change
    (B) reaches
    (C) reached
    (D) will reach

    Ⓐ Ⓑ Ⓒ Ⓓ

2. Each of the people standing in line at the Department of Motor Vehicles <u>was</u> waiting to talk to the shift supervisor.

    (A) No change
    (B) were
    (C) had been
    (D) have been

    Ⓐ Ⓑ Ⓒ Ⓓ

3. The book of matches <u>was laying</u> on the counter.

    (A) No change
    (B) was lying
    (C) were laying
    (D) were lying

    Ⓐ Ⓑ Ⓒ Ⓓ

4. Despite having eaten a huge dinner, <u>a craving for popcorn came over Robert</u> at the movie.

    (A) No change
    (B) a craving for popcorn comes over Robert
    (C) Robert got a craving for popcorn
    (D) Robert was getting a craving for popcorn

    Ⓐ Ⓑ Ⓒ Ⓓ

5. <u>Hopefully,</u> I'll pass my driving test on the first try.

   (A) No change   (C) Hoping,

   (B) I hoped   (D) I hope

Ⓐ Ⓑ Ⓒ Ⓓ

6. When I got to my grandmother's house, she asked me if I <u>had eaten</u> earlier.

   (A) No change   (C) hadn't eaten

   (B) ate   (D) was eating

Ⓐ Ⓑ Ⓒ Ⓓ

7. I turned the TV on just in time to hear the commentator <u>talking on</u> the conflict in Europe.

   (A) No change   (C) talking to

   (B) talking of   (D) talking about

Ⓐ Ⓑ Ⓒ Ⓓ

8. Anna studied both geometry rules and Spanish prepositions on Wednesday, and was afraid she wouldn't remember <u>them</u> on Thursday.

   (A) No change

   (B) either the rules or the prepositions

   (C) either of them

   (D) her

Ⓐ Ⓑ Ⓒ Ⓓ

9. All the students edited <u>his or her</u> own papers.

   (A) No change   (C) their

   (B) she or he   (D) theirs

Ⓐ Ⓑ Ⓒ Ⓓ

10. Once the family moved to a larger apartment, Kyra's two sons each had <u>his</u> own room.

   (A) No change   (C) his or her

   (B) their   (D) one's

Ⓐ Ⓑ Ⓒ Ⓓ

11. Bob asked Ken to get <u>his</u> coat from the closet.

    (A) No change   (C) a

    (B) Ken's   (D) their

    Ⓐ Ⓑ Ⓒ Ⓓ

12. I laughed when I found out that my brother got a ticket for driving <u>too slow</u>.

    (A) No change   (C) slowly enough

    (B) slower   (D) too slowly

    Ⓐ Ⓑ Ⓒ Ⓓ

13. She did so <u>well</u> on the paper that she didn't have to take the final exam.

    (A) No change   (C) goodly

    (B) good   (D) excellent

    Ⓐ Ⓑ Ⓒ Ⓓ

14. <u>The women</u> ate her sandwich and then threw her napkin in the garbage can.

    (A) No change   (C) The man

    (B) The men   (D) The woman

    Ⓐ Ⓑ Ⓒ Ⓓ

15. The rising cost of tuitions at private high schools in the area <u>is forcing</u> many parents to send their children to public high schools.

    (A) No change   (C) is forced

    (B) are forcing   (D) are forced

    Ⓐ Ⓑ Ⓒ Ⓓ

16. <u>Each citizen</u> of the country should save for his or her own retirement, instead of depending on Social Security.

    (A) No change   (C) Each one of the citizens

    (B) All citizens   (D) Many citizens

    Ⓐ Ⓑ Ⓒ Ⓓ

17. Every year we <u>rode</u> our bikes in the St. Patrick's Day Road Race in March.

   (A) No change   (C) are riding
   (B) ride   (D) had ridden

   Ⓐ Ⓑ Ⓒ Ⓓ

18. In his latest essay he <u>has argued</u> that the Big Bang Theory is incorrect.

   (A) No change   (C) argues
   (B) argue   (D) was arguing

   Ⓐ Ⓑ Ⓒ Ⓓ

19. My neighbor asked me <u>to have fed</u> her cat while she was away on vacation.

   (A) No change   (C) is feeding
   (B) feed   (D) to feed

   Ⓐ Ⓑ Ⓒ Ⓓ

20. Don't <u>be asking</u> me the same questions over and over.

   (A) No change   (C) you asks
   (B) ask   (D) to ask

   Ⓐ Ⓑ Ⓒ Ⓓ

21. The movie in which Bill Murray keeps reliving the same day over and over again <u>is</u> one of my favorite movies.

   (A) No change   (C) has
   (B) are   (D) had

   Ⓐ Ⓑ Ⓒ Ⓓ

22. Her performance wasn't <u>energetically enough</u> to win the talent show.

   (A) No change   (C) energetic enough
   (B) so energetic as   (D) as energetic enough

   Ⓐ Ⓑ Ⓒ Ⓓ

23. The book review criticized the author <u>most unfair</u> for taking elements from *Moby Dick*.

(A) No change
(B) unfair
(C) as unfairly
(D) unfairly

Ⓐ Ⓑ Ⓒ Ⓓ

24. As people age, <u>his or her</u> personality traits become more pronounced.

(A) No change
(B) their
(C) our
(D) whose

Ⓐ Ⓑ Ⓒ Ⓓ

25. Because of the increasing pollution in the lake, there were <u>less than</u> fish than there had been ten years earlier.

(A) No change
(B) less
(C) fewer as
(D) fewer

Ⓐ Ⓑ Ⓒ Ⓓ

26. I need <u>an hand</u> with this box; it's too heavy for me to carry by myself.

(A) No change
(B) a hand
(C) the hand
(D) some hands

Ⓐ Ⓑ Ⓒ Ⓓ

27. The economic policies of the United States don't always make sense, even to the people who created <u>it</u>.

(A) No change
(B) these
(C) those
(D) them

Ⓐ Ⓑ Ⓒ Ⓓ

28. The car, <u>who</u> was only a year old, needed a new transmission.

(A) No change
(B) which
(C) they
(D) whom

Ⓐ Ⓑ Ⓒ Ⓓ

29. Students don't always like their teachers because <u>they</u> don't usually show their personalities at school.

    (A) No change   (C) the teachers

    (B) them   (D) them teachers

    Ⓐ Ⓑ Ⓒ Ⓓ

30. My friend had to choose between going to college <u>and</u> going to Spain.

    (A) No change   (C) but

    (B) or   (D) nor

    Ⓐ Ⓑ Ⓒ Ⓓ

31. Sending a paper by email is <u>as fast than</u> sending it by fax.

    (A) No change   (C) so fast as

    (B) faster than   (D) as faster as

    Ⓐ Ⓑ Ⓒ Ⓓ

32. Alicia was driving down the road when she heard her favorite song <u>in</u> the radio.

    (A) No change   (C) from

    (B) onto   (D) on

    Ⓐ Ⓑ Ⓒ Ⓓ

33. Widely <u>known to as</u> an expert on moths, Dr. Kaczynski just completed her first book.

    (A) No change   (C) knowing about

    (B) known as   (D) known to

    Ⓐ Ⓑ Ⓒ Ⓓ

34. <u>Although</u> many people think there should be a city-wide curfew, I disagree.

    (A) No change   (C) In spite of

    (B) As   (D) Because

    Ⓐ Ⓑ Ⓒ Ⓓ

35. This theme has been developed in the works of major authors <u>like</u> Austen, Wharton, and Fitzgerald.

    (A) No change   (C) as
    (B) such as   (D) numbering

    Ⓐ Ⓑ Ⓒ Ⓓ

36. The sofa was upholstered in <u>real</u> leather.

    (A) No change   (C) more real
    (B) really   (D) realized

    Ⓐ Ⓑ Ⓒ Ⓓ

37. Our local newspaper published an account <u>the controversial school board meeting</u>.

    (A) No change
    (B) of the controversial school board meeting
    (C) for the controversial school board meeting
    (D) from the controversial school board meeting

    Ⓐ Ⓑ Ⓒ Ⓓ

38. <u>Whose</u> spices in the sauce caused my mother's tongue to swell.

    (A) No change   (C) The
    (B) A   (D) An

    Ⓐ Ⓑ Ⓒ Ⓓ

39. No matter how <u>many</u> money he made, he never forgot his impoverished childhood.

    (A) No change   (C) less
    (B) few   (D) much

    Ⓐ Ⓑ Ⓒ Ⓓ

40. My parents' house is <u>older than one</u> on their block.

    (A) No change   (C) the older of
    (B) the oldest one   (D) oldest than any

    Ⓐ Ⓑ Ⓒ Ⓓ

EXERCISE 2

Directions: Read each paragraph. Then, answer the questions that follow.

1. (1) Once I realized that I had to improve my study habits, I decided to ask for help. (2) I asked my English teacher if she could help me make a plan to learn better study skills. (3) Once I had followed the plan for several weeks, my grades started to improve. (4) I've been on the honor roll now for the last five quarters.

   Where in the paragraph should the following sentence be inserted?

   I used her plan and practiced every night at home while I did my homework.

   (A) Between sentences 1 and 2

   (B) Between sentences 2 and 3

   (C) Between sentences 3 and 4

   (D) After sentence 4

   Ⓐ Ⓑ Ⓒ Ⓓ

2. (1) When I was 12, I broke my leg by falling out of a tree. (2) I climbed the tree because my cousin dared me to do it. (3) He was really surprised that I made it all the way to the top, but not as surprised as I was when I lost my grip. (4) The last thing I remember before I hit the ground is looking at the branch in my hand and realizing it wasn't attached to the tree anymore.

   Where in the paragraph should the following sentence be inserted?

   The only consolation was that my cousin was grounded for the entire six weeks my leg was in a cast.

   (A) Between sentences 1 and 2

   (B) Between sentences 2 and 3

   (C) Between sentences 3 and 4

   (D) After sentence 4

   Ⓐ Ⓑ Ⓒ Ⓓ

CHAPTER
6

PT/HSPA, FCAT, MEAP HST, MCAS, GEE21, Regents Exams, SOL, NCCT, AHSGE, GHSGT,
NCCT, AHSGE, GHSGT, BST, BSAP, WASL, CAHSEE, TAAS, OGT /HSPA, FCAT, MEA
GT, HSPT/HSPA, FCAT, MEAP HST, MCAS, GEE21, Regents Exams NCCT, AHSGE, G

3. (1) My grandmother had a disease that made her lose her eyesight. (2) I remember the first time I visited her and she couldn't see me anymore. (3) It made me feel bad that things would never be the way they used to be when we made her special cookies together. (4) I thought I saw her crying, but she wiped away the tears when she heard me come into the room.

Where in the paragraph should the following sentence be inserted?

I think it made her sad about that, too.

(A) Between sentences 1 and 2

(B) Between sentences 2 and 3

(C) Between sentences 3 and 4

(D) After sentence 4

Ⓐ Ⓑ Ⓒ Ⓓ

4. (1) My family has always been very close to each other. (2) My dad worked for a company that transferred him to 6 different cities in thirteen years. (3) I've lived in nine different houses, and gone to seven different schools, so it was hard to make new friends so many times. (4) It just seemed to make more sense to make friends with my parents and with my two sisters.

Where in the paragraph should the following sentence be inserted?

If I had to pick only one reason for this I would say it is because we moved around so much when I was growing up.

(A) Between sentences 1 and 2

(B) Between sentences 2 and 3

(C) Between sentences 3 and 4

(D) After sentence 4

Ⓐ Ⓑ Ⓒ Ⓓ

WRITING

5. (1) I never understood why my aunt cried whenever she heard the song "Besame Mucho" on the radio. (2) One day I asked my mother, and she explained that my grandfather used to sing that song every morning while he shaved before he went to work. (3) She'd sing along and pretend to play the violin. (4) After my grandfather died, my aunt couldn't listen to that song without thinking about all the good times they'd shared.

Where in the paragraph should the following sentence be inserted?

My aunt used to sit on the laundry hamper and watch him shave.

(A) Between sentences 1 and 2

(B) Between sentences 2 and 3

(C) Between sentences 3 and 4

(D) After sentence 4

ⒶⒷⒸⒹ

6. (1) In my "Life Skills" class, we had to pretend to be single parents for a week. (2) We each had to carry around a doll with a 10-pound sack of flour for a body. (3) Lots of kids thought it was going to be fun, but it turned out to be a ton of work. (4) And if we left the doll someplace without someone watching it or if the sack of flour broke open, we flunked the project automatically.

Where in the paragraph should the following sentence be inserted?

The doll got really heavy to carry around all the time, and if we wanted a break we had to hire a babysitter.

(A) Between sentences 1 and 2

(B) Between sentences 2 and 3

(C) Between sentences 3 and 4

(D) After sentence 4

ⒶⒷⒸⒹ

7. (1) My parents found my dog on their front porch when she was a puppy. (2) I was only 4, so we've really grown up together. (3) She thinks I'm her own personal human; she waits for me every day by the door and barks when I come in. (4) I may just have to bring her along and take her to classes with me.

Where in the paragraph should the following sentence be inserted?

I don't know what's going to happen when I move out to go to college.

(A) Between sentences 1 and 2

(B) Between sentences 2 and 3

(C) Between sentences 3 and 4

(D) After sentence 4

Ⓐ Ⓑ Ⓒ Ⓓ

8. (1) When I was 5, my sister tricked me into eating dirt. (2) She mixed dirt and water and made brownies out of mud. (3) I didn't think they smelled like real brownies, but she told me that she made them in the microwave instead of the oven, and that's why they didn't smell like chocolate. (4) What a nasty surprise it was when I bit into one and it was just mud.

Where in the paragraph should the following sentence be inserted?

I can still feel the way the dirt felt grinding around in my teeth.

(A) Between sentences 1 and 2

(B) Between sentences 2 and 3

(C) Between sentences 3 and 4

(D) After sentence 4

Ⓐ Ⓑ Ⓒ Ⓓ

9. (1) I've always wanted to be an emergency medical technician, or EMT. (2) I would pretend to drive it, and then jump out to give mouth-to-mouth resuscitation to our dog. (3) The dog really hated that and would run away. (4) My brother still likes to tease me about that sometimes.

Where in the paragraph should the following sentence be inserted?

When my parents got a new refrigerator, my mom gave me the box it came in to make my own pretend ambulance.

(A) Between sentences 1 and 2

(B) Between sentences 2 and 3

(C) Between sentences 3 and 4

(D) After sentence 4

Ⓐ Ⓑ Ⓒ Ⓓ

10. (1) I have always known that I'm adopted. (2) It's not that hard to figure out, since both my parents have blond hair and blue eyes, and I have black hair and brown eyes. (3) It always seemed so strange when people would ask if they were my "real" parents. (4) I always answered, "I can touch them, so they must be real."

Where in the paragraph should the following sentence be inserted?

It was never a big deal to us, but some people just didn't seem to understand so they asked stupid questions.

(A) Between sentences 1 and 2

(B) Between sentences 2 and 3

(C) Between sentences 3 and 4

(D) After sentence 4

Ⓐ Ⓑ Ⓒ Ⓓ

11. (1) The first job I ever had was mowing lawns. (2) I started when I was 12 by asking my neighbors if they would pay me to mow their lawns every Saturday. (3) The neighbor on the left side of my house lets his lawn grow too long before he cuts it. (4) I eventually got five regular weekly customers, who each paid me $10. (5) After I paid my dad $.50 per lawn for the use of his mower, I still had a nice profit of $47.50 a week.

Which of the sentences in the paragraph above should be deleted for being off-topic?

(A) 2 **(C)** 4

(B) 3 **(D)** 5

Ⓐ Ⓑ Ⓒ Ⓓ

12. (1) I have known for several years that I do not want to have children of my own. (2) My main motivation for this decision is to help prevent overcrowding of the planet. (3) So many of our current problems are caused by over-crowding and competition for resources that it just doesn't make sense to make more people. (4) My sister disagrees and wants to have at least three children. (5) I might consider adopting children, but only because this wouldn't add to the population explosion.

Which of the sentences in the paragraph above should be deleted for being off-topic?

(A) 2 **(C)** 4

(B) 3 **(D)** 5

Ⓐ Ⓑ Ⓒ Ⓓ

13. (1) I have already completed the first part of my plan to become a surgeon. (2) To get into a good medical school, I will need to attend a good college, so I will need to earn the best grades I can in high school. (3) With that in mind, I have been studying as hard as I can for the past three years. (4) Lots of my friends go to parties and neglect their work unless they have a test the next day. (5) This studying has paid off, because I have a 3.96 grade point average.

Which of the sentences in the paragraph above should be deleted for being off-topic?

(A) 2

(B) 3

(C) 4

(D) 5

(A)(B)(C)(D)

14. (1) The best argument I can think of for starting the school day an hour later is based on science. (2) Scientists have shown that teenagers need more sleep than either children or adults. (3) Babies need the most sleep of all, but teenagers are second. (4) Teenagers are also hard-wired to fall asleep later at night than children do. (5) This means that the only time they can get this extra sleep is in the morning.

Which of the sentences in the paragraph above should be deleted for being off-topic?

(A) 2

(B) 3

(C) 4

(D) 5

(A)(B)(C)(D)

15. (1) It is an extremely unpopular view among people my age, but I feel that the driving age should be increased to 18 years. (2) I find that my opinions are often different than those of other people my age. (3) Since drivers under the age of 18 have a higher percentage of accidents, which we know is true because insurance companies charge teenage drivers more than adults, it makes sense not to allow teenagers to drive. (4) By raising the age to get a license to 18, we would allow people to mature for another few years before we trust them with an automobile, which is a lethal weapon. (5) I realize that there are some 16-year-olds who are mature

enough to drive responsibly, but many more do not have good enough judgment to be trusted with a car.

Which of the sentences in the paragraph above should be deleted for being off-topic?

(A) 2 (C) 4
(B) 3 (D) 5

Ⓐ Ⓑ Ⓒ Ⓓ

16. (1) Recycling paper, metal, glass, and plastic should be mandatory throughout the United States. (2) The energy spent on recycling existing materials is no greater than that used to make new ones. (3) The impact on the environment of reusing old materials instead of using even more natural resources is great, however. (4) In addition, recycling helps reduce the problem of where to store all our garbage.
(5) Composting our kitchen scraps also helps the environment.

Which of the sentences in the paragraph above should be deleted for being off-topic?

(A) 2 (C) 4
(B) 3 (D) 5

Ⓐ Ⓑ Ⓒ Ⓓ

17. (1) The best experience I ever had volunteering happened when I was reading at the nursing home. (2) I used to go there every Wednesday after school and read to some of the residents who couldn't see well enough to read to themselves anymore. (3) One senior citizen named Rose always asked me to read letters from her granddaughter. (4) Her granddaughter lived in New York City. (5) One time, however, the card she asked me to read was really a thank-you card from Rose to me.

Which of the sentences in the paragraph above should be deleted for being off-topic?

(A) 2 (C) 4
(B) 3 (D) 5

Ⓐ Ⓑ Ⓒ Ⓓ

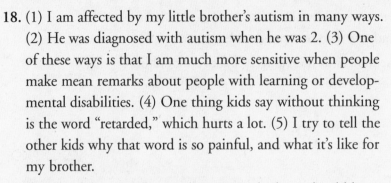

18. (1) I am affected by my little brother's autism in many ways. (2) He was diagnosed with autism when he was 2. (3) One of these ways is that I am much more sensitive when people make mean remarks about people with learning or developmental disabilities. (4) One thing kids say without thinking is the word "retarded," which hurts a lot. (5) I try to tell the other kids why that word is so painful, and what it's like for my brother.

Which of the sentences in the paragraph above should be deleted for being off-topic?

(A) 2   (C) 4

(B) 3   (D) 5

Ⓐ Ⓑ Ⓒ Ⓓ

19. (1) I grew up speaking Russian in my house. (2) My parents still speak to me only in Russian, even though they both speak English really well. (3) They both have accents, but you can still understand everything they say in English. (4) It's just one small way we try to preserve the culture my parents grew up in. (5) I thought all American kids spoke a different language at home with their families until I got to grade school and found out that most of the other kids only spoke English.

Which of the sentences in the paragraph above should be deleted for being off-topic?

(A) 2   (C) 4

(B) 3   (D) 5

Ⓐ Ⓑ Ⓒ Ⓓ

20. (1) Many fast-food companies are deliberately misleading in their ads. (2) They show their burgers with beautiful tomatoes and crisp green lettuce to make us think they give us at least a serving of vegetables. (3) The actual burger you get from the store, however, usually only has a tiny piece of lettuce and a white piece of tomato. (4) Instead of a serving of vegetables, we're really getting a serving of fatty meat and a soggy bun. (5) Eating vegetables is important because they prevent many diseases like cancer and heart disease.

Which of the sentences in the paragraph above should be deleted for being off-topic?

(A) 2   **(C)** 4

(B) 3   **(D)** 5

Ⓐ Ⓑ Ⓒ Ⓓ

21. (1) I think all companies should be required to give their employees cost-of-living raises every year. (2) While this would cost the companies more money than just keeping wages the same, it would help the employees. (3) In the end, it would help the companies, because with more money to spend, employees would put more money into the economy and into the companies. (4) In some industries, the "real" wage has gone down over the past twenty years because wages haven't gone up but expenses like housing, food, and clothes have. (5) This is not right, and the government should force companies to give raises every year.

Which of the following changes would improve the paragraph above?

(A) Delete sentence 2

(B) Switch sentences 2 and 5

(C) Put sentence 3 after sentence 5

(D) Put sentence 4 after sentence 1

Ⓐ Ⓑ Ⓒ Ⓓ

22. (1) Deciding whether or not to buy an air conditioner can be a tough decision. (2) On one hand, people need to be cool when it is extremely hot in the summer. (3) If they are too hot, they could have health problems and will not be productive at their jobs. (4) On the other hand, air conditioners use a lot of electricity, which wastes natural resources. (5) In addition, many older air conditioners release Freon, a dangerous chemical, into the environment.

Which of the following changes would improve the paragraph above?

(A) No change

(B) Switch sentences 3 and 4

(C) Delete sentence 5

(D) Put sentence 4 after sentence 1

Ⓐ Ⓑ Ⓒ Ⓓ

23. (1) One career I would never want to have would be a dentist. (2) Although I am interested in many areas of science, I think I would be just too disgusted if I had to look inside other people's mouths all day. (3) Frankly, I also don't think I'd be any good at it. (4) The worst cases would be people who smoked and had extremely yellow teeth, or people who didn't brush their teeth and had decaying cavities. (5) I would never be able to fix any cavities by using the drill, since the sound makes me wince.

Which of the following changes would improve the paragraph above?

(A) No change

(B) Switch sentences 3 and 4

(C) Put sentence 3 after sentence 5

(D) Remove sentence 2

Ⓐ Ⓑ Ⓒ Ⓓ

24. (1) I don't think that figure skating should be classified as a "sport." (2) There is no doubt that it requires a tremendous amount of athletic talent to be a figure skater, but this doesn't mean that it is a sport. (3) A sport is an athletic contest in which the winner is chosen objectively, either by scoring the most points, or by doing something the farthest or fastest. (4) Figure skating is judged based on opinion, so it is not a sport. (5) I still think it should be in the Olympics, though.

Which of the following changes would improve the paragraph above?

(A) Put sentence 1 after sentence 4

(B) Delete sentence 4

(C) Delete sentence 5

(D) Switch sentences 3 and 4

Ⓐ Ⓑ Ⓒ Ⓓ

25. (1) Anyone who wants to have a baby should be required to take classes and pass a written test on what to do and not to do with children. (2) So many parents, both teenagers and adults, do not seem to know what children should and shouldn't do. (3) A baby should only be drinking its mother's milk or formula, not sugary soda. (4) One example of this is that last week I saw a lady giving her baby orange soda to drink. (5) If she had been forced to take a class on basic nutrition for babies, she wouldn't have done this.

Which of the following changes would improve the paragraph above?

(A) No change

(B) Switch sentences 3 and 4

(C) Delete sentence 2

(D) Put sentence 5 after sentence 1

Ⓐ Ⓑ Ⓒ Ⓓ

26. (1) If I won the lottery I would invest most of the money, but I would also give some of it away. (2) I would give some of it to my aunt and uncle, who have to take care of their daughter Lina, who is disabled. (3) I know that they worry about how she will be able to survive once they are gone, so I would give them enough money that they wouldn't have to worry about Lina. (4) To me, this would be as good as investing my money in stocks, because it would be an investment in my family. (5) I think families have an obligation to take care of each other.

Which of the following changes would improve the paragraph above?

(A) No change

(B) Delete sentence 4

(C) Switch sentences 3 and 5

(D) Put sentence 5 after sentence 1

Ⓐ Ⓑ Ⓒ Ⓓ

27. (1) If I could be any animal I would be a dolphin. (2) I would be a dolphin because they are beautiful and smart. (3) Scientists say, in fact, that dolphins may be as smart as humans are. (4) I would love to be able to roam the oceans observing all the forms of life that we never see here on land. (5) The biggest danger of being a dolphin would be pollution of the oceans.

Which of the following changes would improve the paragraph above?

(A) No change

(B) Combine sentences 1 and 2

(C) Switch sentences 3 and 4

(D) Delete sentence 2

Ⓐ Ⓑ Ⓒ Ⓓ

28. (1) Some people say that baseball is our national pastime. (2) I don't agree with this statement, because not very many people can play baseball, and there are plenty of Americans who don't even like to watch it. (3) Maybe this statement is just old-fashioned and doesn't reflect the way things are in modern times. (4) For instance, my mother and her friends have absolutely no interest in baseball, and they are "typical Americans." (5) There are just too many other things to be interested in now that we have the technology to find out about them.

Which of the following changes would improve the paragraph above?

(A) No change

(B) Delete sentence 2

(C) Put sentence 5 after sentence 2

(D) Switch sentences 3 and 4

Ⓐ Ⓑ Ⓒ Ⓓ

29. (1) If given the choice between a well-paying job that I didn't like and a job I loved that didn't pay well, I would choose the well-paying job. (2) Then, I would quit and do what I liked to do. (3) I would work at it for long enough to save up enough money to live on for a few years. (4) By saving up all that money ahead of time, I'd be able to do what I liked without worrying about earning enough to support myself. (5) This way I would completely enjoy the experience without any added pressure.

Which of the following changes would improve the paragraph above?

(A) Switch sentences 2 and 3

(B) Put sentence 5 after sentence 3

(C) Delete sentence 3

(D) Delete sentence 5

Ⓐ Ⓑ Ⓒ Ⓓ

30. (1) My dream is to be a rock musician. (2) I don't even care about being famous; I just want to be able to support myself playing bass guitar. (3) I've been playing in bands since I was 13. (4) Even if I never make it big I'll continue to play for the rest of my life. (5) My other dream is to own a classic Corvette.

Which of the following changes would improve the paragraph above?

(A) No change

(B) Combine sentences 1 and 2

(C) Delete sentence 5

(D) Switch sentences 4 and 5

Ⓐ Ⓑ Ⓒ Ⓓ

Multiple-Choice Exercises

Directions: Read the following student-written essay. Then, answer the questions that follow. These exercises are similar to those you may see on your state's exit-level exam.

(1) I remember the day I knew I wanted to be a teacher; I was in 9th grade, and I was having <u>issues with</u> algebra. (2) I never thought I was real good at math. (3) I always did fine though. (4) But algebra was harder for me, and I had to work to keep my grades up. (5) How could I ever make it through Geometry? (6) Then, one day, a student in my class asked if I could help him figure out the lesson.

(7) At first I said I couldn't get it either. (8) He seemed very frustrated, so I said I'd give it a try. (9) To explain it to him, I tried to remember what the teacher had said, and I just said that. (10) The other student tried to do a problem right then, and I couldn't believe it when he was done. (11) He got the right answer! (12) After I saw his success with that problem. (13) <u>I tried some problem's myself</u>, and I got them all right. (14) I felt good that I was able to help him, and I was surprised to find out that teaching is a good way to learn. (15) I decided then and there that teaching was the career for me.

SPT/HSPA, FCAT, MEAP HST, MCAS, GEE21, Regents Exams, SOL, NCCT, AHSGE, GHSGT,
L, NCCT, AHSGE, GHSGT, BST, BSAP, WASL, CAHSEE, TAAS, OGT, T/HSPA, FCAT, ME
OGT, HSPT/HSPA, FCAT, MEAP HST, MCAS, GEE21, Regents Exams, NCCT, AHSGE, C

CHAPTER
6

1. How is <u>issues with</u> in sentence 1 *best* rewritten to be more specific?

   (A) disputes over   (C) questions about

   (B) difficulty with   (D) worry over

   Ⓐ Ⓑ Ⓒ Ⓓ

2. Which of the following is not a sentence?

   (A) 7   (C) 11

   (B) 8   (D) 12

   Ⓐ Ⓑ Ⓒ Ⓓ

3. Which of the following sentences is the least relevant to the story?

   (A) 5   (C) 8

   (B) 7   (D) 13

   Ⓐ Ⓑ Ⓒ Ⓓ

4. Sentence 9 is best written:

   (A) I tried to remember, and explain just like the teacher did.

   (B) As I explained it to him, I tried to remember exactly what the teacher said in class.

   (C) To explain it to him, I just said what the teacher said, when I could remember.

   (D) As it is

   Ⓐ Ⓑ Ⓒ Ⓓ

5. In sentence 13, <u>I tried some problem's myself</u> is correctly written:

   (A) I try some problem's myself

   (B) I try some problems myself

   (C) I tried some problems myself

   (D) As it is

   Ⓐ Ⓑ Ⓒ Ⓓ

Directions: Read the following student-written essay. Then, answer the questions that follow.

(1) My younger brother thought he was stupid. (2) He had difficulty understanding his teachers, struggling with his homework, and frequently failed tests. (3) Then, one year he was <u>tested and had</u> a learning disability. (4) Since he had trouble reading, the school gave him a reader for his tests. (5) The reader would read all of the questions and answers out loud to him so that his reading problem wouldn't interfere with his ability to get right answers.

(6) Once he began taking tests with the reader, he started getting As and Bs! (7) <u>Doing well on tests made a big difference</u> in his self-esteem as well as in his grade point average. (8) He realized that he was just as smart as anyone else. (9) I saw how frustrating it had been for someone when they understand the material but couldn't prove it on a test. (10) This made me aware that everyone learns differently; I, for instance, would have a terrible time taking a test with a reader; I'm just lucky that most tests are written.

6. Sentence 2 could best be written:
   (A) He had difficulty understanding his teachers, struggling with his homework, and frequently failing tests.
   (B) He had difficulty to understand his teachers, struggle with his homework, and frequently fail tests.
   (C) He had difficulty understanding his teachers, struggled with his homework, and frequently failed tests.
   (D) As it is

Ⓐ Ⓑ Ⓒ Ⓓ

7. In sentence 3, how could <u>tested and had</u> be rewritten to make more sense?
   (A) tested and got
   (B) tested for and got
   (C) tested for and found to have
   (D) tested for and having

Ⓐ Ⓑ Ⓒ Ⓓ

8. In sentence 7, how could <u>Doing well on tests made a big difference</u> be rewritten most clearly?

   (A) Taking tests with the reader made a big difference

   (B) It made a big difference

   (C) The learning disability made a big difference

   (D) As it is

   Ⓐ Ⓑ Ⓒ Ⓓ

9. Sentence 9 is best written:

   (A) I saw how frustrating it is for someone to understand the material, but be unable to prove it on a test.

   (B) I saw how frustrating it was for someone who understands the material and can't prove it on a test.

   (C) I saw how frustrating it would be to be in understanding of the material but also unable to prove it on a test.

   (D) As it is

   Ⓐ Ⓑ Ⓒ Ⓓ

10. Sentence 10 could best be written:

   (A) This made me aware that everyone learns differently. I, for instance, would have a terrible time taking a test with a reader; I'm just lucky that most tests are written.

   (B) This made me aware that everyone learns differently, I, for instance, would have a terrible time taking a test with a reader, I'm just lucky that most tests are written.

   (C) This made me aware that everyone learns differently; I for instance would have a terrible time taking a test with a reader; I'm just lucky that most tests are written.

   (D) As it is

   Ⓐ Ⓑ Ⓒ Ⓓ

Directions: Read the following student-written essay. Then, answer the questions that follow.

(1) Former U.S. president Grover Cleveland <u>supposably said</u>, "What do you think American people would think about me if I wasted my time going to a ballgame?" (2) For a small group of college professors, however, baseball is anything but a waste of time. (3) Though some of their colleagues are condescending toward them. (4) These professors believe that one of America's most popular <u>pastimes are food</u> for serious thought. (5) As it turns out, <u>baseball and it's history</u> are intimately connected with American history.

(6) Many social and cultural trends can be traced along with the development of baseball and the impact it has had on our society. (7) Baseball is more popular even than football. (8) Race relations, corporate business, labor, and transportation are just some of the phenomena that can be viewed through the lens of baseball. (9) Of course, one great side benefit for a <u>Professor of baseball</u> is that he or she can use a childhood passion as the fuel for an adult career.

11. In sentence 1, <u>supposably said</u> is correctly written:
    (A) supposably once said
    (B) supposably says
    (C) supposedly said
    (D) supposedly says

Ⓐ Ⓑ Ⓒ Ⓓ

12. Sentences 3 and 4 are best written:

  (A) Though some of their colleagues are condescending toward them; these professors believe that one of America's most popular pastimes are food for serious thought.

  (B) Though some of their colleagues are condescending toward them, these professors believe that one of America's most popular pastimes is food for serious thought.

  (C) Though some of their colleagues, are condescending toward them. These professors believe, that one of America's most popular pastimes, is food for serious thought.

  (D) Though some of their colleagues are condescending. Toward them, these professors believe that one of America's most popular pastimes are food for serious thought.

Ⓐ Ⓑ Ⓒ Ⓓ

13. In sentence 4, <u>pastimes are food</u> is best written:

  (A) pastimes is food

  (B) pasttimes are food

  (C) pastimes are foods

  (D) pastimes were food

Ⓐ Ⓑ Ⓒ Ⓓ

14. In sentence 5, <u>baseball and it's history</u> is best written:

  (A) baseball and its history

  (B) baseball, and it's history

  (C) baseball and it's history's

  (D) As it is

Ⓐ Ⓑ Ⓒ Ⓓ

15. Which of the following sentences is least relevant to the essay?

  (A) 6   (C) 8

  (B) 7   (D) 9

Ⓐ Ⓑ Ⓒ Ⓓ

Directions: Read the following student letter. Then, answer the questions that follow.

18 Daisy Lane
McKees Rocks, PA 15234
May 8, 2002

Mr. Donald Bernstein
Head Counselor
Camp Sloan
485 River's Gate Drive
Erie Park, PA 16187

Dear Mr. Bernstein,

I am writing to apply for the Assistant Art Teacher position you advertised in the camp newspaper. I always loved attending Camp Sloan when I was in grade school, and have particularly benefited from the arts and crafts program. I would enjoy the opportunity to share my creativity with younger children.

I feel that I am qualified to help teach this program because I am very experienced with crafts, children, and Camp Sloan. The last two years I attended camp I was chosen as an <u>Art Leader, I</u> helped keep track of supplies and clean up after arts and crafts sessions. I also volunteered to run creative workshops at the Arts Festival in <u>Down Town</u> Pittsburgh last summer.

I am creative and patient. I truly enjoy seeing how much fun children have when they make, build, and draw. <u>I can't never think</u> of anything I like better than helping to make art fun for kids. I think it's important to encourage <u>every kid's</u> inner artist.

If you need personal references, you can contact Ms. Barbara Blaine, <u>whom was my supervisor last summer</u>, and Mr. Timothy Allen, my guidance counselor.

Please contact me at your convenience if you have any questions or to schedule an interview. Thank you very much for your time and consideration.

Sincerely,
Mandy Plin

16. The last two years I attended camp I was chosen as an <u>Art Leader, I</u> helped keep track of supplies and clean up after arts and crafts sessions.

    How is <u>Art Leader, I</u> correctly written?

    (A) Art Leader I   (C) Art Leader and I

    (B) Art Leader; I   (D) As it is

    Ⓐ Ⓑ Ⓒ Ⓓ

17. I also volunteered to run creative workshops at the Arts Festival in <u>Down Town</u> Pittsburgh last summer.

    How is <u>Down Town</u> correctly written?

    (A) Down town   (C) Downtown

    (B) downtown   (D) As it is

    Ⓐ Ⓑ Ⓒ Ⓓ

18. <u>I can't never think</u> of anything I like better than helping to make art fun for kids.

    How is <u>I can't never think</u> correctly written?

    (A) I can't think   (C) I cannot ever think

    (B) I can't ever think   (D) As it is

    Ⓐ Ⓑ Ⓒ Ⓓ

19. I think it's important to encourage <u>every kid's</u> inner artist.

    How is <u>every kid's</u> correctly written?

    (A) every kids'   (C) each children's

    (B) every kids   (D) As it is

    Ⓐ Ⓑ Ⓒ Ⓓ

20. If you need personal references, you can contact Ms. Barbara Blaine, <u>whom was my supervisor last summer</u>, and Mr. Timothy Allen, my guidance counselor.

    How is <u>whom was my supervisor last summer</u> correctly written?

    (A) who was my supervisor last summer

    (B) whose supervised me last summer

    (C) for who I worked last summer

    (D) As it is

    Ⓐ Ⓑ Ⓒ Ⓓ

Directions: Read the following student letter. The underlined word or phrase may not be correct grammatically. Choose the correct answer from the four choices.

1289 Swan Drive
Enfield, AZ 85693
May 8, 2002

Dr. Richard Bartlett
Superintendent
37 Hermitage Blvd.
Enfield, AZ 85693

Dear Dr. Bartlett,

I would like to nominate my voice teacher, Mr. Thomas Groves, for "Teacher of the Year." He has made a big impact on my life and the <u>life of my classmates</u>, and we all agree that he deserves to be recognized.

In order to be in the 7th grade choir, we all had to audition when we were in 6th grade, though everyone made the cut. Even though I was accepted, I was shy about singing, so I didn't put choir on my schedule. Mr. Groves pulled me out of math class one day to ask me to give his class a <u>chance if I</u> didn't like it, I could quit. I agreed to try, but I was skeptical.

This is just an example of the <u>personal interest</u> Mr. Groves takes in his students. In class, he is the most energetic, entertaining, patient, and demanding teacher I've ever had. He won't hesitate to single out someone <u>whose struggling</u>, but he does it in the kindest and funniest way. He uses humor to put people at ease and as a result his students enjoy working very hard to meet his high expectations.

I have attached statements from thirty of <u>my other classmates</u> explaining how Mr. Groves has helped them and why they think he should be "Teacher of the Year." Please contact me if you have any questions. Thank you very much for considering Mr. Groves for this honor.

Sincerely,

Tom Cole

21. He has made a big impact on my life and the <u>life of my classmates</u>, and we all agree that he deserves to be recognized.

    (A) life of my Classmates

    (B) lives of my Class Mates

    (C) lives of my classmates

    (D) No error

    Ⓐ Ⓑ Ⓒ Ⓓ

22. Mr. Groves pulled me out of math class one day to ask me to give his class a <u>chance if I</u> didn't like it, I could quit.

    (A) Mr. Groves pulled me out of math class one day to ask me to give his class a chance and if I didn't like it, I could quit.

    (B) Mr. Groves pulled me out of math class one day to ask me to give his class a chance; if I didn't like it, I could quit.

    (C) Mr. Groves pulled me out of math class one day, to ask me to give his class a chance, if I didn't like it, I could quit.

    (D) No error

    Ⓐ Ⓑ Ⓒ Ⓓ

23. This is just an example of the <u>personal interest</u> Mr. Groves takes in his students.

    (A) personalized interest

    (B) personable interest

    (C) personalizable interest

    (D) No error

    Ⓐ Ⓑ Ⓒ Ⓓ

24. He won't hesitate to single out someone <u>whose struggling</u>, but he does it in the kindest and funniest way.

    (A) whose is struggling

    (B) who's is struggling

    (C) who is struggling

    (D) No error

    Ⓐ Ⓑ Ⓒ Ⓓ

25. I have attached statements from thirty of <u>my other Class-mates</u> explaining how Mr. Groves has helped them and why they think he should be "Teacher of the Year."

    (A) my classmates

    (B) my other classmates

    (C) the other classmates

    (D) No error

    Ⓐ Ⓑ Ⓒ Ⓓ

Directions: Read the following student letter. The underlined word or phrase may not be correct grammatically. Choose the correct answer from the four choices.

To the Editor (of the school newspaper):

As most people already know, the school board has been making some changes. Starting next year, we may face a new <u>schedule, where we go</u> to school <u>for three months, then one month off</u>. They have also changed the dress code for next year. We are not going to be allowed to wear shorts anymore, and we can't wear hats <u>and advertising T-shirts</u>.

Now, we do not really need to wear hats inside, and we do not need to be advertising anything on our clothes. But if we can't wear shorts we really will be <u>effected</u>. Just picture how much you want to put on long pants on a hot summer day and drive to school. And with the new staggered school year, we'll be in school during some of the summer, but not allowed to wear shorts.

If <u>they're</u> going to make us go to school in the summer, they shouldn't have added insult to injury in taking away our right to wear shorts.

Mark Brooks

26. Starting next year, we may face a new <u>schedule, where we go</u> to school for three months, then one month off.

    (A) schedule, we will go

    (B) schedule, that will go

    (C) schedule, requiring us to

    (D) No error

    Ⓐ Ⓑ Ⓒ Ⓓ

27. Starting next year, we may face a new schedule, where we go to school <u>for three months, then one month off.</u>

(A) for three months. Then one month off.

(B) for three months, and then a month off.

(C) for three months, and then we get one month off.

(D) No error

Ⓐ Ⓑ Ⓒ Ⓓ

28. But if we can't wear shorts we really will be <u>effected</u>.

(A) afected   (C) efected

(B) affected   (D) No error

Ⓐ Ⓑ Ⓒ Ⓓ

29. We are not going to be wearing shorts anymore, and we can't wear hats <u>or advertising T-shirts.</u>

(A) or T-shirts with advertising.

(B) and advertising T-shirts.

(C) and advertising in T-shirts.

(D) No error

Ⓐ Ⓑ Ⓒ Ⓓ

30. If <u>they're</u> going to make us go to school in the summer, they shouldn't add insult to injury in taking away our right to wear shorts.

(A) thier   (C) there

(B) their   (D) No error

Ⓐ Ⓑ Ⓒ Ⓓ

Directions: Read the following student-written essay. Then, answer the questions that follow.

(1) "Heads or tails?" (2) This is a question most of us have asked or been asked at some point. (3) For thousands of years, people used coin tosses, drawn straws, and rolled dice when there's a decision we'd rather not have to make. (4) Perhaps we need to figure out who gets the prize, who will take out the garbage, or who sits in the back seat—some things we prefer to decide by chance.

(5) Relying on chance to decide may be done for different reasons. (6) Usually, it has to do with the fact that chance outcomes are random. (7) People think that if a decision is made randomly, then it must be fair. (8) But that depends on the definition of fair. (9) Is it fair to decide by coin toss who will clean the bathroom each week? (10) If the same person might have to do it ten weeks in a row? (11) Of course, over time, each person should win about the same number of times, but their's no guarantee.

(12) Another reason people make decisions by chance is to allow luck or Fate to decide. (13) Different cultures have different ideas about Fate and divine intervention, but throughout human history chance has been used as a way to let luck have a hand in the decision. (14) "Leave it to chance" people say "Let luck decide." (15) People who believe in Fate think the winner of the lottery somehow deserves the money. (16) Whether or not the winner believes in Fate, chances are he or she feels pretty lucky.

(17) Despite the possible rationalizations for dependents on chance in decision-making, as often as not the real reason people "leave it to chance" is expediency. (18) Think of it: you and your camp buddy are trying to decide who gets the last cookie, and your both eager to leave the table to play backgammon (since the winner gets to sleep on the top bunk). (19) You have to decide who gets the cookie before either of you can eat it, and frankly you're sick of arguing about it. (20) What could be easier than a quick coin toss to end the squabble? (21) Even if you can't agree on who gets to eat the cookie, you can decide to accept the decision of an external source (random chance) that doesn't favor either party.

(22) But after all . . . it's just a cookie. (23) When the stakes are really high, most people prefer a more logical approach to the decision, and consensus on the outcome, even if it takes longer to decide. (24) Though people often claim that it's fairness or fate that they rely on, few people leave anything to chance that would really hurt them if they lost. (25) For last cookies, top bunks, front seats, and clean toilets; however, random chance can save a lot of time and hurt feelings.

31. What change, if any, should be made to sentence 3?

    (A) Change *people used* to *people used to*

    (B) Change *people used* to *people had used*

    (C) Change *people used* to *people have used*

    (D) Make no change

    Ⓐ Ⓑ Ⓒ Ⓓ

32. How can sentence 4 be best written?

    (A) Perhaps we need to figure out who will get the prize, who will take out the garbage, or who sits in the back seat—some things we prefer to decide by chance.

    (B) Perhaps we need to figure out who will get the prize, who will take out the garbage, or who will sit in the back seat—some things we prefer to decide by chance.

    (C) Perhaps we need to figure out who gets the prize, who will take out the garbage, or who will sit in the back seat—some things we prefer to decide by chance.

    (D) As it is

    Ⓐ Ⓑ Ⓒ Ⓓ

33. How can sentences 9 and 10 best be written?

    (A) Is it fair to decide by coin toss who will clean the bathroom each week, if the same person might have to do it ten weeks in a row?

    (B) Is it fair to decide by coin toss who will clean the bathroom each week: if the same person might have to do it ten weeks in a row?

    (C) Is it fair to decide by coin toss who will clean the bathroom each week; if the same person might have to do it ten weeks in a row?

    (D) As they are

    Ⓐ Ⓑ Ⓒ Ⓓ

34. What change, if any, should be made to sentence 11?

   (A) Change *their's* to *theirs*

   (B) Change *their's* to *there's*

   (C) Change *their's* to *theirs'*

   (D) Make no change

Ⓐ Ⓑ Ⓒ Ⓓ

35. What change, if any, should be made to sentence 13?

   (A) Change *Fate and divine intervention* to *Fate and Divine intervention*

   (B) Change *Fate and divine intervention* to *Fate and Divine Intervention*

   (C) Change *Fate and divine intervention* to *fate and divine intervention*

   (D) Make no change

Ⓐ Ⓑ Ⓒ Ⓓ

36. Sentence 14 is best written in which of the following ways?

   (A) "Leave it to chance," people say, "Let luck decide."

   (B) "Leave it to chance", people say, "Let luck decide."

   (C) "Leave it to chance", people say "Let luck decide."

   (D) As it is

Ⓐ Ⓑ Ⓒ Ⓓ

37. What change, if any, should be made to sentence 17?

   (A) Change *dependents* to *dependent*

   (B) Change *dependents* to *dependence*

   (C) Change *dependents* to *dependentsy*

   (D) Make no change

Ⓐ Ⓑ Ⓒ Ⓓ

38. What change, if any, should be made to sentence 18?

   (A) Change *your both* to *your all*

   (B) Change *your both* to *you're both*

   (C) Change *your both* to *you're both of you*

   (D) Make no change

Ⓐ Ⓑ Ⓒ Ⓓ

39. What, if any, change should be made to sentence 24?

(A) Change *them if they lost* to *him or her if he or she lost*

(B) Change *them if they lost* to *them if they lost them*

(C) Change *them if they lost* to *he or she if they lost*

(D) Make no change

Ⓐ Ⓑ Ⓒ Ⓓ

40. Sentence 25 could best be written in which of the following ways?

(A) For last cookies, top bunks, front seats, and clean toilets. However, random chance can save a lot of time and hurt feelings.

(B) For last cookies, top bunks, front seats, and clean toilets, however, random chance can save a lot of time and hurt feelings.

(C) For last cookies, top bunks, front seats, and clean toilets, however; random chance can save a lot of time and hurt feelings.

(D) As it is

Ⓐ Ⓑ Ⓒ Ⓓ

Directions: Read the following student-written essay. Then, answer the questions that follow.

(1) "It is a truth universally acknowledged, that a single man in possession of a good fortune, must be in want of a wife." (2) So goes the famous opening line of Jane Austen's *Pride and Prejudice*, and so begins the story of Elizabeth Bennet. (3) Lizzy Bennet is the second oldest of four daughters, none of which are married, and whose mother is very eager to find them good husbands. (4) In early nineteenth-century England, a good husband was by definition well connected and rich.

(5) When Mr. Bingley moves into a nearby estate, Mrs. Bennet became very excited by the idea that he might want to marry one of her girls. (6) Mr. Bennet, on the other hand, thinks his wife is foolish and seems to believe that Lizzy is too good for marriage. (7) This is not surprising, as Mr. and Mrs. Bennet's own troublesome marriage is, throughout the novel, a mockery of the institution that is the focus of all Mrs. Bennet's hopes. (8) In her world, young womens' energy was typically spent trying to snag

a suitable man of fortune, since the prospect of marrying beneath her station—or, worse, not marrying at all—was unthinkable.

(9) Lizzy's sisters and friends seem much more eager to get the marriage matter settled than Lizzy does. (10) Lizzy's cousin, Mr. Collins, comes to visit the Bennet's at one point, and her mother immediately begins to imagine a match between him and Lizzy. (11) Mr. Collins thinks Lizzy would be a great catch, and he begins to woo her shamelessly and without regard for the fact that Lizzy is disinterested. (12) When he proposes to her, she turns him down. (13) To the mortification of her mother, the townspeople, and, most of all, Collins himself. (14) He had felt very sure that she would accept him because a young woman in those days was expected to accept the first offer of marriage that came her way. (15) When Collins' affections and marriage proposals are suddenly transferred to Lizzy's friend Charlotte, that's exactly what she does.

(16) The bulk of the story is devoted to the relationship between Lizzy and Mr. Darcy, Mr. Bingley's haughty friend. (17) Lizzy is obviously independent and would rather remain unmarried rather than marrying someone she could not relate to. (18) Since her relationship with Darcy begins with her hating him and his being the person she could least imagine relating to, she is surprised to eventually realize that he is the best person she could spend the rest of her life with. (19) She didn't start out looking for a husband, but she found one in spite of herself.

(20) Like any Austen novel, *Pride and Prejudice* ends neatly with most of the characters getting married: Collins marries Charlotte, Bingley marries Lizzy's sister Jane, and Lizzy herself marries Darcy. (21) Though in the end Lizzy does the socially excepted thing in getting married, Austen uses Lizzy's independence of thought throughout the story to highlight the frustration experienced by a woman in a society that judged her worth by her ability to marry well.

41. What change, if any, should be made in sentence 3?

(A) Change *whose* to *who's*

(B) Change *which* to *whom*

(C) Change *them* to *each of them*

(D) Make no change

Ⓐ Ⓑ Ⓒ Ⓓ

T/HSPA, FCAT, MEAP HST, MCAS, GEE21, Regents Exams, SOL, NCCT, AHSGE, GHSGT, B NCCT, AHSGE, GHSGT, BST, BSAP, WASL, CAHSEE, TAAS, OGT, T/HSPA, FCAT, MEA GT, HSPT/HSPA, FCAT, MEAP HST, MCAS, GEE21, Regents Exams, NCCT, AHSGE, GH GHSGT, BST, BSAP, WASL, CAHSEE, TAAS, OGT, HSPT/HSPA, FCAT, MEAP HST, MCAS

CHAPTER **6**

WRITING

42. What change, if any, should be made to sentence 21?

   (A) Change *socially excepted* to *socially exceptional*

   (B) Change *socially excepted* to *societally excepted*

   (C) Change *socially excepted* to *socially accepted*

   (D) Make no change

   Ⓐ Ⓑ Ⓒ Ⓓ

43. What change, if any, should be made to sentence 5?

   (A) Change *became* to *becomes*

   (B) Change *became* to *become*

   (C) Change *became* to *would become*

   (D) Make no change

   Ⓐ Ⓑ Ⓒ Ⓓ

44. What change, if any, should be made to sentence 8?

   (A) Change *young womens'* to *young women's*

   (B) Change *young womens'* to *a young woman's*

   (C) Change *young womens'* to *young womans'*

   (D) Make no change

   Ⓐ Ⓑ Ⓒ Ⓓ

45. What change, if any, should be made to sentence 10?

   (A) Change *Bennet's* to *Bennets*

   (B) Change *Bennet's* to *Bennets'*

   (C) Change *him and Lizzy* to *he and Lizzy*

   (D) Make no change

   Ⓐ Ⓑ Ⓒ Ⓓ

46. What change, if any, should be made to sentence 11?

   (A) Change *disinterested* to *misinterested*

   (B) Change *disinterested* to *uninteresting*

   (C) Change *disinterested* to *uninterested*

   (D) Make no change

   Ⓐ Ⓑ Ⓒ Ⓓ

47. What is the most effective way to rewrite the ideas in sentences 12 and 13?

   (A) When he proposes to her, she turns him down; to the mortification of her mother, the townspeople, and, most of all, Collins himself.

   (B) When he proposes to her, she turns him down. To the mortification of her mother, the townspeople, and; most of all Collins himself.

   (C) When he proposes to her, she turns him down; to the mortification of her mother, the townspeople. And most of all Collins himself.

   (D) When he proposes to her, she turns him down, to the mortification of her mother, the townspeople, and, most of all, Collins himself.

Ⓐ Ⓑ Ⓒ Ⓓ

48. What change, if any, should be made to sentence 15?

   (A) Change *she does* to *she did*

   (B) Change *she does* to *Charlotte does*

   (C) Change *she does* to *Charlotte did*

   (D) Make no change

Ⓐ Ⓑ Ⓒ Ⓓ

49. What change, if any, should be made to sentence 17?

   (A) Change *rather than marrying* to *marry*

   (B) Change *rather than marrying* to *rather than marry*

   (C) Change *rather than marrying* to *marrying*

   (D) Make no change

Ⓐ Ⓑ Ⓒ Ⓓ

50. What change, if any, should be made to sentence 18?

   (A) Change *his being* to *him being*

   (B) Change *his being* to *he being*

   (C) Change *his being* to *his been*

   (D) Make no change

Ⓐ Ⓑ Ⓒ Ⓓ

PT/HSPA, FCAT, MEAP HST, MCAS, GEE21, Regents Exams, SOL, NCCT, AHSGE, GHSGT,
NCCT, AHSGE, GHSGT, BST, BSAP, WASL, CAHSEE, TAAS, OGT, HSPA, FCAT, MEA
GT, HSPT/HSPA, FCAT, MEAP HST, MCAS, GEE21, Regents Exam, NCCT, AHSGE, G

CHAPTER
6

Answers and Explanations

EXERCISE 1

1. **The correct answer is (C).** The action of the sentence took place *yesterday*, so the verb must be in the past tense. Only choice (C) contains a verb in the past tense: *reached*.

2. **The correct answer is (A).** The subject of the sentence, *each*, is singular. Therefore, the verb must be singular, so eliminate choice (B). The sentence is in the past tense, so eliminate choice (D). Choice (C) could only be correct if the sentence indicated that the waiting in line took place before something else happened. No other event is mentioned, so you can eliminate choice (C).

3. **The correct answer is (B).** There are two things to look at in this question. The first is the difference between *was* and *were*. The subject of the sentence is the singular noun *book*, not the plural noun *matches*, which is part of a prepositional phrase. Therefore, the correct verb is *was*. Eliminate choices (C) and (D). The other aspect of the question is the difference between *laying* and *lying*. To *lay* means to place something down, while to *lie* means to rest on something. Since the matches were resting on the counter, not placing something else on the counter, the correct answer is *lying*. You can eliminate choice (A).

4. **The correct answer is (C).** The phrase that starts the sentence, "despite having eaten a huge dinner," modifies whatever noun comes immediately after the comma. This means that choices (A) and (B) are saying that the craving had eaten a huge dinner. This makes no sense, so eliminate choices (A) and (B). Choices (C) and (D) say that Robert had eaten a huge dinner, which makes a lot more sense. Choice (C) uses the verb *got*, which indicates that it happened once, while choice (D) uses the verb *was getting*, which indicates that it happened repeatedly or over a period of time. Since the sentence is telling about one episode, it makes sense to say that it happened once only. You can eliminate choice (D).

5. **The correct answer is (D).** The word *hopefully* is an adverb, which means that it modifies a verb. In this case, that verb is *pass*. As written, this sentence says that the author will pass the test in a hopeful manner. This isn't what the sentence should say, so eliminate choice (A). Choice

(B) is in the past tense, which conflicts with the future tense in the rest of the sentence. Eliminate it. In choice (C), *hoping* is a gerund that isn't attached to anything, which is wrong. Eliminate it. In choice (D), *I hope* expresses the author's hope that he or she will pass the test, which is the intention of the sentence.

6. **The correct answer is (A).** In this sentence, the grandmother is asking about an action that happened once and was completed. This calls for the use of the past perfect tense, which is the helper verb *had* plus the past participle form of the verb. In this case it is *had eaten*. Choice (A) is correct. Choice (C) is incorrect because, although it uses the past perfect tense, it introduces a negative for no reason. Choice (B) uses the simple past, which would indicate that the grandmother wondered if the author had ever eaten in the past. Choice (D) is incorrect because *was eating* indicates eating in the present, not the past.

7. **The correct answer is (D).** The idiomatically correct phrase is *talk about*. Therefore, the only correct choice is (D).

8. **The correct answer is (C).** The underlined word or phrase needs to refer to the rules and prepositions. Eliminate choice (A) because *them* isn't specific enough—it could refer to either the rules or the prepositions or both. Choice (B) mentions the rules and prepositions again unnecessarily, so eliminate it. Choice (C) uses the pronoun *them* but specifies that it could be either one. Choice (D) is incorrect because *her* can't refer to the rules or the prepositions.

9. **The correct answer is (C).** The subject of the sentence is *all*, which is plural. Therefore, the underlined word must be a plural pronoun modifying the noun *papers*. Eliminate choices (A) and (B) because they are singular. Eliminate choice (D) because *theirs* can only be used to stand in for a noun, not to modify it.

10. **The correct answer is (A).** The underlined word must be a pronoun modifying the word *room*. Choice (A) is correct because it shows that each room belongs to one boy. Eliminate choice (B) because it changes the meaning to indicate that both boys own one room together. Eliminate choice (C) because two sons are *his*, not *his or her*. Eliminate choice (D) because *one* is used to refer to any person in general, male or female, and in this case, we know the gender of the owners of the rooms.

11. **The correct answer is (B).** Choice (B) is awkward, but it's the only choice that makes the sentence clear. Choice (A) could indicate either

Bob's coat or Ken's coat, and choice (C) could be any coat in the closet. Choice (D) sounds as if Bob and Ken only own one coat between them. The only possible answer is choice (B).

12. **The correct answer is (D).** The underlined word modifies the verb *driving*, so it must be an adverb. Eliminate choices (A) and (B) because they are adjectives. Eliminate choice (C) because no one would get a ticket for doing something *enough*. Instead, they would get a ticket for doing too much of something, which is what choice (D) says.

13. **The correct answer is (A).** The underlined word modifies the verb *did*, so it must be an adverb. Eliminate choices (B) and (D) because they are adjectives. Eliminate choice (C) because *goodly* is actually an adjective, not an adverb, meaning a considerable amount. Choice (A) is the only adverb among the choices.

14. **The correct answer is (D).** The pronoun in the sentence, *her*, takes the place of a singular, feminine noun. Eliminate choices (A) and (B) because they are plural and choice (C) because it is masculine. Choice (D) is the only singular, feminine noun.

15. **The correct answer is (A).** The subject of the sentence is *cost*, which is singular. Eliminate choices (B) and (D) because *are* cannot be used with a singular subject. Eliminate choice (C), because *is forced* makes a passive construction, so the meaning of the sentence would be that the parents force the cost to rise, not that the cost forces the parents to look at other schools. Choice (A) indicates correctly that the cost forces the parents to look at other schools.

16. **The correct answer is (A).** The underlined words need to be a singular noun phrase because the pronoun referring to the underlined words are singular ("his or her"). Eliminate choices (B) and (D) because they are plural. Eliminate choice (C) because it is unnecessarily wordy, especially compared with choice (A), which says the same thing with only half the words.

17. **The correct answer is (B).** The words *every year* indicate that riding the bikes is a habitual or repeated action. Therefore, the present tense of the verb should be used to indicate that this takes place regularly. Choices (A), (C), and (D) are not present tense, so they should be eliminated. Choice (B) is in the present tense.

18. **The correct answer is (C).** The underlined verb must be either the present or past simple tense, because the author either did or does some-

thing in the essay. Eliminate choices (A) and (D) because they are not simple tense. Eliminate choice (B) because *argue* doesn't agree with the subject *he*. Choice (C) is correct because *argues* matches *he*.

19. **The correct answer is (D).** The correct form of the expression is "to ask to do" something. Therefore, the correct answer is (D), *to feed*. Eliminate choices (A), (B), and (C) because they don't follow the format of the expression.

20. **The correct answer is (B).** The constructions *do not* or *don't* must be followed by the present tense of a verb. Choice (B) is the present tense of the verb, so eliminate choices (A), (C), and (D).

21. **The correct answer is (A).** The underlined word must be a form of the verb *to be*, so eliminate choices (C) and (D), which are forms of the verb *to have*. The underlined word must agree with the subject *movie*, which is singular. Eliminate choice (B) because *are* is a plural verb. Choice (A) is singular.

22. **The correct answer is (C).** The underlined word modifies the noun performance, so it must be an adjective. Eliminate choice (A) because it is an adverb. Eliminate choice (B) because the construction "so . . . as" doesn't make sense in this sentence. Choice (C) is correct because it contains an adjective and the adverb *enough*, which modifies *energetic*. Eliminate choice (D) because the construction "as . . . enough" is incorrect.

23. **The correct answer is (D).** The underlined word modifies the verb *criticized*, so it must be an adverb. Eliminate choices (A) and (B) because they are adjectives. Eliminate choice (C) because the construction "as . . . for" is incorrect. Choice (D) is an adverb.

24. **The correct answer is (B).** The underlined word needs to be a pronoun referring to the plural noun *people*. Eliminate choice (A) because it is not plural. Choice (B) correctly refers to *people*. Eliminate choice (C) because there is no indication that the author is trying to refer to himself as part of the group of people in the sentence. Eliminate choice (D) because *whose* is an adjective, not a pronoun.

25. **The correct answer is (D).** The underlined word describes the number of fish in the lake. Since fish are countable, *less* is incorrect and *fewer* is correct. Eliminate choices (A) and (B) for using *less*. Eliminate choice (C) because this would make the phrase say "fewer as . . . than," which is incorrect. Choice (D) uses *fewer* correctly.

26. **The correct answer is (B).** The idiomatic expression is *a hand*. Also, *an* is generally only used before *h* to precede vowel sounds, as in "He is *an* honest man" or "It would be *an* honor." Eliminate choices (A), (C), and (D).

27. **The correct answer is (D).** The underlined word is a pronoun taking the place of the plural subject of the sentence, *policies*. Eliminate choice (A) because it is singular. Eliminate choices (B) and (C) because they both need to modify another noun not take the place of one. Choice (D) correctly takes the place of the plural subject.

28. **The correct answer is (B).** The underlined word modifies *car*. Eliminate choices (A) and (D) because a car is not a person. Eliminate choice (C) because a car is not plural. Choice (B) is singular and refers to an inanimate object.

29. **The correct answer is (C).** The underlined word must refer specifically to the teachers. Eliminate choice (A) because it could refer to either the teachers or the students. Eliminate choice (B) because *them* must be an object, not a subject. Choice (C) refers only to the teachers. Eliminate choice (D) because "them teachers" is incorrect, since *them* must be an object, not a modifier.

30. **The correct answer is (A).** The underlined word must complete the phrase "between A and B." The only word that fits is *and*, so eliminate choices (B), (C), and (D) and choose choice (A) as the correct answer.

31. **The correct answer is (B).** The meaning of the sentence is that a comparison between e-mail and fax produces one clear winner. Therefore, eliminate choices (A), (C), and (D) because they incorrectly attempt to say that the two are equal. The only choice that indicates a comparison and is also grammatically correct is choice (B).

32. **The correct answer is (D).** The idiomatically correct prepositional phrase is "on the radio." Eliminate choices (A), (B), and (C), and choose choice (D) as the correct answer.

33. **The correct answer is (B).** The idiomatic expression is "known as," so eliminate choices (A), (C), and (D).

34. **The correct answer is (A).** The underlined word needs to indicate that the clause before the comma and the clause after the comma are conflicting. Eliminate choices (B) and (D), because the words *as* and *because* indicate that the clauses are similar. Eliminate choice (C) because

the phrase "in spite of" must be followed either by a gerund or by the words "the fact that." Choice (A) indicates that the clauses conflict.

35. **The correct answer is (B).** The underlined word introduces the examples of authors who developed the theme. The word *like* means *similar to*, and *such as* means *for example*. In this case, the authors are examples of authors who developed the theme, not just authors who were similar to the ones who developed the theme, so eliminate choice (A). Choice (B) is correct. Eliminate choice (C) because *as* cannot stand alone in this case. Eliminate choice (D) because it doesn't matter how many authors there were, which is what *numbering* indicates.

36. **The correct answer is (A).** The underlined word modifies the noun *leather*, so it must be an adjective. Eliminate choice (B) because *really* is an adverb. Eliminate choice (C) because there is nothing to compare the couch to, so there is no need for the word *more*. Eliminate choice (D) because, when used as an adjective, *realized* means "successfully completed," not *genuine*.

37. **The correct answer is (B).** The phrase "the controversial school board meeting" needs to begin with a preposition. Eliminate choice (A). The correct idiom is "account of," so the correct answer is (B), and you can eliminate choices (C) and (D).

38. **The correct answer is (C).** The underlined word must be an article. Choice (A) is an adjective, so eliminate it. Since the sentence is referring to specific spices, the article must be *the*. So, eliminate choices (B) and (D).

39. **The correct answer is (D).** The underlined word needs to modify *money*. Since *money* is not countable, choices (A) and (B) are not correct. "How less money" doesn't make any sense, so eliminate choice (C). "Much money," choice (D), is correct.

40. **The correct answer is (B).** The underlined phrase compares the author's parents' house to all the other houses on their block. When comparing three or more things we use the superlative (*-est*) form, so eliminate choices (A) and (C). The superlative form *oldest* used with "than any" in choice (D) is incorrect. Choice (B) uses the superlative form correctly, "the oldest."

PT/HSPA, FCAT, MEAP HST, MCAS, GEE21, Regents Exams, SOL, NCCT, AHSGE, GHSGT,
, NCCT, AHSGE, GHSGT, BST, BSAP, WASL, CAHSEE, TAAS, OGT, T/HSPA, FCAT, MEA
GT, HSPT/HSPA, FCAT, MEAP HST, MCAS, GEE21, Regents Exams, NCCT, AHSGE, G

CHAPTER
6

WRITING

EXERCISE 2

1. **The correct answer is (B).** The missing sentence should go between sentences 2 and 3 in the paragraph. Sentence 2 talks about asking the teacher to make a study plan, while sentence 3 discusses the results of having used the plan. This means that the information in the missing sentence about using the plan every night should go between them.

2. **The correct answer is (D).** The missing sentence should go after sentence 4, at the end of the paragraph. The missing sentence discusses what happened to the author and the author's cousin after the author fell out of the tree, so it needs to go after the author fell out of the tree, which happens in sentence 4.

3. **The correct answer is (C).** The missing sentence should go between sentences 3 and 4. Sentence 3 talks about how the author was sad. The missing sentence states that the grandmother was sad, too. The *too* shows that it has to go after the sentence about the author being sad, or sentence 3. The missing sentence also introduces the idea that the grandmother was sad to explain why she was crying in sentence 4.

4. **The correct answer is (A).** The missing sentence refers to sentence 1 when it says "reason for this," so it must come after sentence 1. It also introduces the idea that the family moved around a lot, so it must come before sentence 2.

5. **The correct answer is (B).** The missing sentence refers to the grandfather as *him*, so it must come after the grandfather is mentioned in sentence 2. It also introduces the idea that the aunt watched the grandfather shave. Sentence 3 states that *she* would sing along, but doesn't say who *she* is, so the missing sentence needs to come before sentence 3 to make it obvious that *she* is the aunt.

6. **The correct answer is (C).** The missing sentence tells why the project was so difficult—the doll was heavy and they couldn't take a break—so it needs to come after sentence 3, which says that the project was hard. It needs to come before sentence 4, which talks about flunking the project.

7. **The correct answer is (C).** The only logical place the missing sentence can go is between sentence 3, which talks about the special relationship the author and the dog have, and sentence 4, which states that the au-

thor may have to "bring her along." Without the missing sentence, we don't know where the author intends to bring the dog.

8. **The correct answer is (D).** The missing sentence should go after sentence 4. Sentence 4 describes the author biting into the mud, and the missing sentence describes the way it tasted once it was in the author's mouth.

9. **The correct answer is (A).** The missing sentence has to go before sentence 2, since otherwise there would be no way for us to know what the author was referring to by "drive it." The missing sentence makes it clear that "it" was the pretend ambulance.

10. **The correct answer is (B).** The missing sentence should go between sentences 2 and 3. The missing sentence discusses dumb questions that people asked the author, and sentence 3 gives an example of one of these questions.

11. **The correct answer is (B).** Sentence 3 should be deleted. The paragraph is about the author's job mowing lawns and how she or he started and built up the business. Sentence 3 talks about a neighbor's lawn, but it doesn't directly relate to the author's business.

12. **The correct answer is (C).** Sentence 4 should be removed, because the topic of the paragraph is the author's opinion on having children. The author's sister's opinion is irrelevant to the topic.

13. **The correct answer is (C).** Sentence 4 should be removed. The topic of the paragraph is how the author studies hard to get good grades, so the author's friends' study habits don't have anything to do with the topic.

14. **The correct answer is (B).** Sentence 3 should be removed. The paragraph discusses teenagers' increased need for sleep, so babies' need for sleep is off-topic.

15. **The correct answer is (A).** Sentence 2 should be removed, because it has nothing to do with the author's argument that the driving age should be raised. Whether or not the author usually agrees with others of the same age doesn't have any effect on this argument.

16. **The correct answer is (D).** Sentence 5 should be removed. The topic of the paragraph is mandatory recycling, so composting kitchen scraps doesn't have anything to do with the topic.

17. **The correct answer is (C).** Sentence 4 should be removed. The para-

HSPT/HSPA, FCAT, MEAP HST, MCAS, GEE21, Regents Exams, SOL, AHSGE, GHSGT,
NCCT, AHSGE, GHSGT, BST, BSAP, WASL, CAHSEE, TAAS, OGT, HSPA, FCAT, MEAP
GT, HSPT/HSPA, FCAT, MEAP HST, MCAS, GEE21, Regents Exams, NCCT, AHSGE, G
GHSGT, BST, BSAP, WASL, CAHSEE, TAAS, OGT, HSPT/HSPA, FCAT, MEAP HST, MCAS

CHAPTER
6

graph tells a story about the author's volunteer experience. The grand-daughter is mentioned in passing, but where she lived is not important to the story and just diverts attention from the surprise ending.

18. **The correct answer is (A).** Sentence 2 should be removed. Sentence 1 states that the author has been affected in many ways, and sentence 3 begins with "one of these ways." Sentence 2 disturbs the flow of the paragraph. In addition, it does not matter to the story when the brother was diagnosed.

19. **The correct answer is (B).** Sentence 3 should be removed. The topic of the paragraph is that the author's family speaks Russian at home to preserve their culture. Stating that the parents only speak Russian at home even though they could speak English adds to the idea that they are doing it deliberately to preserve their culture, but describing their accents doesn't show that their culture is preserved.

20. **The correct answer is (D).** Sentence 5 should be removed. The topic of the paragraph is the difference between burger ads and burger reality. The health benefits of vegetables are off-topic to the paragraph.

21. **The correct answer is (C).** Choice (A) is incorrect because deleting sentence 2 would remove the idea that increasing wages would help employees, so sentence 5 would no longer make sense. Choice (B) is incorrect because sentence 5 would say "this is not right" about the topic sentence of the paragraph (saying that your topic sentence isn't right is not a good way to prove your point). Choice (C) is correct because then the first part of the paragraph would talk about the benefits to the employees and then the end of the paragraph would describe benefits to the companies as well. Choice (D) is incorrect because sentence 5 would say "this is not right" about the benefits of increasing wages to the companies.

22. **The correct answer is (A).** The paragraph flows well as it is written, with arguments for buying an air conditioner first and arguments against it second. Choice (B) is incorrect because this would put a reason for buying an air conditioner directly after the statement against it. Choice (C) is incorrect because there is no need to removed sentence 5. It supports the idea in sentence 4. Choice (D) is incorrect because it makes no sense to say "on the other hand" before you say "on one hand."

23. **The correct answer is (B).** Choice (A) is incorrect, since sentence 3 doesn't make sense where it is in the paragraph. Choice (B) is correct

because this switch would put the reasons the author would be disgusted at the beginning of the paragraph and the idea that the author wouldn't be a good dentist at the end of the paragraph. Choice (C) is incorrect because sentence 3 introduces the idea that the author would be a bad dentist and sentence 5 gives an example of that. Putting the example before the idea wouldn't make sense. Choice (D) is incorrect because then there would be no indication that the author was disgusted by other people's mouths.

24. **The correct answer is (C).** Choice (A) is incorrect because moving the topic sentence of the paragraph would confuse it. Choice (B) is incorrect because sentence 4 states why judging figure skating is different from the author's definition of "sport," and therefore why the author's argument is valid. Choice (C) is correct because whether or not the author wants figure skating in the Olympics has nothing to do with the argument that it is not a sport. Choice (D) is incorrect because switching these sentences would only have a minor effect on the logic in the paragraph, so it wouldn't improve the paragraph (but it also wouldn't really hurt it).

25. **The correct answer is (B).** Choice (A) is incorrect because sentence 3 follows up on the example in sentence 4. Choice (B) is correct because sentence 3 follows up on the example in sentence 4, so they should be switched to make sense. Choice (C) is incorrect because sentence 2 states that the reason they should take classes is because many parents don't know what to do. Otherwise we don't know why the author thinks parents should take classes. Choice (D) is incorrect because *she* in sentence 5 wouldn't refer to anything in sentence 1.

26. **The correct answer is (A).** The paragraph flows well as it is. Choice (B) is incorrect because eliminating sentence 4 wouldn't improve the paragraph. Sentence 4 uses the word *investment* in a way that was not indicated at the beginning of the paragraph and adds to the richness of the paragraph. Choice (C) is incorrect because sentence 3 needs to follow sentence 2 to complete the story of Lina and her parents. Choice (D) is incorrect because sentence 1 does not indicate that the author would give money to a family member, so sentence 5 doesn't make sense there. Sentence 5 only makes sense once we know that the author intends to give money to family members.

27. **The correct answer is (B).** Choice (A) is incorrect because the paragraph would flow better if sentences 1 and 2 were combined into one

sentence saying, "If I could be any animal I would be a dolphin, because they are beautiful and smart." Choice (B) is correct because the paragraph would flow better if sentences 1 and 2 were combined into one sentence saying, "If I could be any animal I would be a dolphin, because they are beautiful and smart." Choice (C) is incorrect because sentence 3 builds upon the idea in sentence 2 that dolphins are smart, so sentence 3 needs to come immediately after sentence 2. Choice (D) is incorrect because sentence 2 introduces the reason the author would like to be a dolphin, which is the point of the paragraph.

28. **The correct answer is (D).** Choice (A) is incorrect because sentence 4 is an example proving that sentence 2 is true, so sentence 4 should immediately follow sentence 2. Choice (B) is incorrect because sentence 2 is the thesis statement of the paragraph. Without it, the paragraph does not make any sense. Choice (C) is incorrect because sentence 4 is an example proving that sentence 2 is true, therefore sentence 4 should immediately follow sentence 2, so sentence 5 cannot immediately follow sentence 2. Choice (D) is correct because sentence 4 is an example proving that sentence 2 is true, so sentence 4 should immediately follow sentence 2.

29. **The correct answer is (A).** Choice (A) is correct because sentence 3 discusses working at the job and saving money, while sentence 2 talks about quitting the job. You have to work at a job before you quit it, so sentence 3 must come before sentence 2. Choice (B) is incorrect because moving sentence 5 would make it sound as if the author would enjoy the job she or he didn't like. Choice (C) is incorrect because deleting sentence 3 would remove the motivation for working at the well-paying job. Choice (D) is incorrect because removing this sentence wouldn't have a huge effect on the paragraph, but sentences 2 and 3 definitely need to be switched.

30. **The correct answer is (C).** Choice (A) is incorrect because sentence 5 is off-topic, since it isn't about the author's dream of being a musician. Choice (B) is incorrect because sentence 2 is already two independent clauses joined by a semicolon. There's no way to combine it with sentence 1 without creating a run-on sentence. Choice (C) is correct because sentence 5 is off-topic, since it isn't about the author's dream of being a musician. Choice (D) is incorrect because sentence 5 is off-topic, since it isn't about the author's dream of being a musician, so it shouldn't be in the paragraph, let alone come before sentence 4.

WARM-UP AND MULTIPLE-CHOICE EXERCISES

MULTIPLE-CHOICE EXERCISES

1. **The correct answer is (B).** The point of this sentence is that algebra was harder for the author than other math classes had been. "Issues with" is very vague and is not formal enough for a written essay, whereas "difficulty with" is the most specific of all the choices and says exactly what the author means—algebra was hard. The author may have had disputes over, questions about, or worry over algebra as well, but none of those helps tell this story.

2. **The correct answer is (D).** The word *after* signals that this is a descriptive clause meant to modify a sentence. Without a subject and predicate to modify this is a sentence fragment (e.g., "*After* I saw his success with that problem, I tried one on my own").

3. **The correct answer is (A).** This story is about learning and developing a desire to teach, and it is told through an experience with algebra. Geometry has nothing to do with the story as a whole.

4. **The correct answer is (B).** As it is, sentence 9 is wordy and confusing. There is an extra comma after *remember*, and "I said just that" is clumsy and informal. Choice (A) does not indicate that the author tried to explain it to another student—it sounds like the author was trying to explain it to the teacher. Choice (B) is much more clear and direct. Choice (C) sounds as if the author couldn't always remember what the teacher had said, which isn't indicated by the rest of the paragraph. Choice (D) doesn't fix the confusing wording. So, choice (B) is the best answer.

5. **The correct answer is (C).** *Problems* is plural, not possessive, so there is no apostrophe. This means choices (A) and (D) can be eliminated. Since the story is written in the past tense, the verb *to try* should be in the past tense also—*tried* instead of *try*. Eliminate choice (B). The only choice left is (C).

6. **The correct answer is (C).** The phrases separated by the commas should have parallel verbs. It's important to understand which part of the sentence is the verb and which part is just there to modify the verb. In the first part of the sentence, *had difficulty* is the verb, not *understanding*, so the verbs in the subsequent phrases should be past tense. He "had difficulty (understanding his teachers), struggled (with his homework), and (frequently) failed tests."

7. **The correct answer is (C).** When combining two facts into one sen-

High Stakes: Writing

tence, each one needs to make sense on its own. As it is, the author is saying, "one year he was tested" and, "one year he had a learning disability." What the author means to say in this case is that, "one year he was *tested for* a learning disability" and, "one year he was *found to have* a learning disability."

8. **The correct answer is (D).** As it is, the sentence is very clear about what affected the author's brother's self-esteem.

9. **The correct answer is (A).** As it is, sentence 9 is a mess of unparallel verb tenses. In choice (A), "to understand" is parallel with "(to) be unable." Also, though in speech people often say "it is frustrating when . . .," in writing it is better to say exactly what is frustrating; in this case, "to understand the material but be unable to prove it on a test."

10. **The correct answer is (A).** As it is, sentence 10 is really three sentences joined together with two semicolons; this should never happen. It could be divided into two sentences (with one semicolon) or even three separate sentences.

11. **The correct answer is (C).** *Supposably* is not a word, though it is a common mispronunciation of *supposedly*.

12. **The correct answer is (B).** "Though some of their colleagues are condescending toward them" is not a sentence. As such, it is properly set off from sentence 4 with a comma.

13. **The correct answer is (A).** The subject of this sentence is *one*, which is singular and takes the singular verb *is*.

14. **The correct answer is (A).** *Its* is the correct possessive form of *it*. *It's* is the contracted form of "it is."

15. **The correct answer is (B).** The popularity of football relative to baseball has nothing to do with baseball as an academic subject.

16. **The correct answer is (B).** "The last two years I attended camp I was chosen as an Art Leader" and "I helped keep track of supplies and clean up after arts and crafts sessions" are actually 2 separate sentences. Joining two sentences with a comma, as in the letter, is called a "comma fault." Two related sentences such as these should always be joined with a semicolon, as in choice (B).

17. **The correct answer is (B).** *Downtown* is one word. Capitalization is reserved for proper nouns such as names of places, such as Pittsburgh.

Generic words that do not refer to any specific named person, place, or thing are not capitalized. Therefore, downtown is not capitalized.

18. **The correct answer is (A).** Since *can't* and *never* are both negative, "can't never" is a double negative. Double negatives are redundant and should be avoided. Choices (B) and (C), while not grammatically incorrect, are unnecessarily wordy.

19. **The correct answer is (D).** "Every kid" is singular; therefore, to make it possessive you need to add an apostrophe and an *s,* as in *kid's.* If you were saying "I think it's important to encourage all kids' inner artists," where *kids* is plural, you would simply add an apostrophe after the *s,* as in *kids'.*

20. **The correct answer is (A).** When choosing between *who* and *whom,* remember that *who* is for subjects and *whom* is for objects. If you're not sure which is which, try substituting the name in that part of the sentence: "Barbara Blaine was my supervisor last summer." Barbara Blaine is the subject, so use *who.*

21. **The correct answer is (C).** *Classmates* is plural, so you must use the plural of *life,* which is *lives.* Also, *classmates* is one word. Capitalization is reserved for proper nouns, such as names of places. Generic words that do not refer to any specific named person, place, or thing are not capitalized. Therefore, *classmates* is not capitalized.

22. **The correct answer is (B).** "If I didn't like it, I could quit" is a new sentence. Tacking it on to the previous sentence with no punctuation creates what is called a "fused sentence," which is grammatically incorrect and confusing to the reader. You could put a period after *chance,* or you could use a semicolon, as in choice (B). You cannot use a comma between the sentences, as in choice (C); to do so is called a "comma fault."

23. **The correct answer is (D).** The issue here is one of word choice, and *personal* aptly describes the kind of interest Mr. Groves took: he made a personal effort with individual students. His actions could be said to have been *personalized* to the needs of the author, but his *interest* was *personal.*

24. **The correct answer is (C).** *Whose* is the possessive form of *who,* not the contraction for *who is.* You could either use *who's* or *who is,* as in choice (C). Choice (B) doesn't work because "who's is struggling" doesn't make sense.

25. **The correct answer is (A).** The author used *other* to say "other than myself," but actually the word *other* here suggests that there was some original group of classmates who didn't write statements, but these "other classmates" did. When you just say "my classmates," it is implied that you don't include yourself. Also, *classmates* is one word. Capitalization is reserved for proper nouns, such as names of places. Generic words that do not refer to any specific named person, place, or thing are not capitalized. Therefore, *classmates* is not capitalized.

26. **The correct answer is (C).** Though in speech, people will naturally say, *where* in this sentence, it is probably short for *wherein*, which would be correct. But the word *where* designates place, and a schedule isn't a place. Among the given choices, only choice (C) does not introduce new errors.

27. **The correct answer is (C).** Based on the phrase, "we go to school for three months," one expects the following phrase to be parallel in construction, with a slight variation in meaning. For parallel structure, the phrase "then one month off" would require the pronoun *we*, as in, "we go . . . then we get . . . ."

28. **The correct answer is (B).** Only the word spelled with an *a* can mean what the author wants it to mean here, namely, influenced, or feeling the effects. *Effected* has a completely different meaning: "caused to happen," as in, "we hope the full change in dress code will not be effected."

29. **The correct answer is (A).** Choice (A) correctly clears up the grammatical ambiguity in the original phrase. The phrase "advertising T-shirts" could refer to T-shirts with advertising on them, or it could refer to students who are engaged in advertising T-shirts (i.e., T-shirts for sale). Choice (C) is also less ambiguous than the original, but it introduces a new problem; it introduces the noun *advertising* such that it is not parallel to the verb in *can't*. When the present participle (an *-ing* verb, like *advertising*) is used as a noun, it is called a gerund.

30. **The correct answer is (D).** *They're* is the contraction of *they are*, as in, "If they are going to make us go to school . . . ." The other choices include correct spellings of *there* and *their*, plus a misspelling of *their*, none of which fits here.

31. **The correct answer is (C).** Since the point is that people still do use chance to make decisions, the author means "people have used." As is, sentence 3 implies that people used chance in the past but don't any longer.

32. **The correct answer is (B).** The verb tenses in all 3 phrases separated by the commas must match: "will get," "will take out," and "will sit."

33. **The correct answer is (A).** Sentence 10 is not a sentence at all but a dependent clause; therefore, the correct way to join it to sentence 9 is with a comma.

34. **The correct answer is (B).** *There's* is the correct contraction of "there is."

35. **The correct answer is (C).** Initial capital letters are for proper names, not general concepts like fate and divine intervention.

36. **The correct answer is (A).** If a quotation appears at the beginning of a sentence, there should always be a comma inside the end quote (unless the quote ends in a question mark or an exclamation point, in which case the existing punctuation should be left and no comma added). If a quotation appears at the end of a sentence, there should always be a comma immediately after the preceding text.

37. **The correct answer is (B).** *Dependence* is the proper spelling of the state of depending on something, though it is pronounced exactly the same way as *dependents*, which is the plural form of *dependent*. "Dependentsy" is a misspelling of *dependency*, which is another acceptable way of saying *dependence*.

38. **The correct answer is (B).** *You're* is the correct contraction of "you are," whereas *your* is the possessive form of the pronoun *you*. In choice (C), "of you" is needlessly repetitive.

39. **The correct answer is (D).** "Few people" is plural and takes the plural form of the pronouns: *them* and *they*. In choice (B), the extra *them* is superfluous and doesn't refer to anything.

40. **The correct answer is (B).** When it is not separating two complete sentences, *however* should be set off with two commas and no semicolons. Choice (A) creates a sentence fragment and a sentence and, thus, is incorrect.

41. **The correct answer is (B).** *Which* is used to refer to inanimate objects; *whom* is better for referring to people.

42. **The correct answer is (C).** *Excepted* means "left out," and *exceptional* means "rare or different from the norm."

SPT/HSPA, FCAT, MEAP HST, MCAS, GEE21, Regents Exams, SOL, NCCT, AHSGE, GHSGT
, NCCT, AHSGE, GHSGT, BST, BSAP, WASL, CAHSEE, TAAS, OGT, HSPA, FCAT, ME
OGT, HSPT/HSPA, FCAT, MEAP HST, MCAS, GEE21, Regents Exams, NCCT, AHSGE, C

CHAPTER
6

43. **The correct answer is (A).** The tenses need to match, so since Bingley *moves* into the neighborhood, Mrs. Bennet *becomes* very excited.

44. **The correct answer is (B).** For parallel structure, "a young woman" would try to snag "a husband." The correct possessive form of *woman* is *woman's*.

45. **The correct answer (A).** Saying Collins came to visit "the Bennet's" begs the question: "the Bennet's . . . *what*?"—what possession belonging to the Bennet family was he there to visit? He came to visit the Bennet family, not one of their possessions, properly pluralized as "the Bennets." Also, "him and Lizzy" is correct as the object of the preposition *between*.

46. **The correct answer is (C).** There are two definitions of *interested*. The more common usage is how people feel when they find something interesting or want to pursue something. If you don't find something interesting or aren't interested in pursuing it, you are not interested in it, or *uninterested*. The other definition means having a personal stake in something, or to be affected by the outcome. If you don't have a stake in something or it does not affect you in any way personally, you are not interested in it, in this case *disinterested*. As Lizzy clearly has a personal stake in whom she chooses to marry, we have to assume the author means that she is *uninterested* in marrying Collins. It would also work to say she is "not interested."

47. **The correct answer is (D).** As it is, sentence 13 is not a sentence at all but rather a prepositional phrase meant to modify sentence 12. Choice (D) has a lot of commas, but this is the correct way to punctuate the phrases that are all modifying the sentence, "She turns him down."

48. **The correct answer is (B).** As it is, it is not clear whether "she" refers to Lizzy or to Charlotte. *Charlotte* is the antecedent in this case, and to make this clear, the author should repeat the name, as in choice (B). *Does* is fine, as the tense matches the tense in "proposals *are* suddenly transferred."

49. **The correct answer is (A).** There are two issues in this sentence: the repetition of the word *rather*, and unparallel verb tense. *Remain* is the present-tense verb we have to match, so we'd choose *marry*.

50. **The correct answer is (D).** It is a common mistake to use *him* in this case, but *his* is the accepted usage.

CHAPTER 7

WRITING EXERCISES

This chapter is divided into two sections. The first is called "Prewriting Exercises." Complete these exercises before you move on to the second section, "Writing Exercises." There are scoring guides and sample brainstorming ideas included in this chapter.

Prewriting Exercises

Exercise 1

For each topic, spend 10 minutes brainstorming and writing a loose outline. If there are two or more sides to a topic, repeat the exercise until you've come up with an outline for each side. There are sample outlines beginning on page 169.

1. Without art, life is meaningless.

2. A person should choose the career that will pay the most.

3. No one is an island.

4. You can tell what the ideals of a society are by the way it treats children.

5. All high school students should be required to volunteer a certain number of hours if they want to graduate.

6. People today are less polite than they were in the past.

7. Movies and television producers pay more attention to advertisers than they do to the public.

8. Society could decrease the level of crime by providing high school students with classes on self-esteem and leadership.

9. People, no matter what religion or culture they belong to, have the same core beliefs.

10. It is better to ask forgiveness after you have done something than permission before you do it.

11. For many students, leaving high school and entering college or the work force will completely change the social rules they have been living with for the past few years. What, in your opinion, is the best way to navigate a new social situation?

12. Some people say that the United States should become more aggressive in mediating disputes in other parts of the world, while others think the United States should focus more on domestic problems. If you could decide what the United States should do, what would be the three most important decisions you would make and why?

13 What are the qualities that make a person a genius? How can we tell the difference between a true genius and a very smart person?

14 Assume that you have a job that pays you more than enough to live on and meet your basic needs. What would you do with the excess money you made? Would you save it or spend it and why?

15 Do you think that different generations can ever understand each other's experiences? If so, how? If not, why?

16 What are the most important qualities to you in a work situation? What would your ideal job consist of?

17 What do you think are the most important values that parents should teach their children? Why?

18 Think about the person you consider your major role model. What qualities does this person have that makes you want to emulate him or her?

19 How do you define patriotism? Does the definition of patriotism depend on the system of government within a given country? Explain.

20 What do you think are the principal skills you will need to become a success in life?

21 Tell about why you feel proud of your heritage. If you aren't proud of your heritage, explain why.

22 If you could see into the future, what are some of the changes you think we will see in the world in the next fifty years?

23 What do you think a child's responsibility is to his parents, if any?

24 Do you think a politician's primary responsibility is to vote according to his own will, or the will of the constituents who elected him? Why?

25 Do you think there are any occupations for which one gender is more suited than the other? Why or why not?

Exercise 2

Now, go back through the topics above. Look at your brainstorming outline for each topic and choose any one point from that outline. Write a paragraph based on that single point. Write as if it were intended to be placed in the middle of the essay, as one of the body paragraphs. There are sample paragraphs beginning on page 178.

Prewriting Sample Responses

Exercise 1: Sample Brainstorming Ideas

[1] Without art, life is meaningless.

Pros:

- Art provides relief from the daily grind.
- People can express their true feelings through art.
- Art provides a way to communicate with others that goes beyond words.

Cons:

- You don't have to be an artist or art fan to be of service to others or to enjoy life.
- Communication between two people is just as valuable as art is to share feelings.
- People can express their feelings in many ways that aren't considered "art."

[2] A person should choose the career that will pay the most.

Pros:

- People have a duty to maximize their education by choosing the career that pays the most, based on their qualifications.
- Choosing a high-paying career will allow them to save for retirement to avoid being a burden on their families.
- Higher salaries contribute more to society through taxes.

Cons:

- A person has a duty to do what makes him or her happy and fulfilled, regardless of money.
- A person in a lower-paying career can save just as much money if she or he doesn't spend as much as a person in a higher-paying career.

- Choosing a low-paying career may contribute more to society by filling valuable occupations like teaching or social work.

3 No one is an island.

Pros:

- Everyone needs other people, even if it's an auto mechanic to fix the person's car.
- Without contact with others, a person will become lonely and depressed.
- The greatest joys in life come from forming relationships with others.

Cons:

- People should work to become self-reliant as much as possible.
- The more independent a person is, the less a burden on society he or she is.
- The most powerful, wealthy people are usually the most independent.

4 You can tell what the ideals of a society are by the way it treats its children.

Pros:

- A society that values children tends also to value the elderly, poor, ill, and mentally ill.
- A society that abandons children tends to be more violent.
- Since children learn to act the way people treat them, it's a never-ending circle.

Cons:

- Some societies love children but don't treat women well.
- Society can treat children harshly because it values order, but not be violent as a whole.
- Many abuses of children are a secret from the overall society, which doesn't have the same values as the abusers.

5 All high school students should be required to volunteer a certain number of hours if they want to graduate.

Pros:

- Education should teach kindness and empathy, as well as reading and math.

- The attitudes and perspectives of students will be improved by volunteering to help people less fortunate than they are.
- A school community will be kinder and more motivated if everyone volunteers.

Cons:

- If students are forced to do it, it's not really volunteering.
- Students will only develop bad attitudes about helping others by being forced to volunteer.
- The people receiving the help may feel bad because the volunteers don't really want to help them.

6 People today are less polite than they were in the past.

Pros:

- Life moves faster, so there's no time for social politeness.
- We have more contact with strangers, so there's no motivation to be nice to people you'll never see again.
- The increasing divide between the rich and poor makes people feel entitled or resentful, so they are meaner.

Cons:

- Technology, such as e-mail and mobile phones, helps us connect with others and be more polite.
- Less formal language and changing social customs do not mean we're not polite, just not as formal.
- We see more people, so we have more bad encounters, but they aren't representative of everyone.

7 Movies and television producers pay more attention to advertisers than they do to the public.

Pros:

- Media is increasingly violent because violence sells more products.
- Programming is created around things that will sell, like action figures.
- Wholesome family programming is considered to be uncool, so advertisers don't support it, and it doesn't get made.

Cons:

- Violence only sells products because the public wants to watch it, so it's really the public's decision.
- Shows and movies with more family-oriented themes don't get large audiences.
- Advertisers only choose their campaigns based on public opinion studies.

8 Society could decrease the level of crime by providing high school students with classes on self-esteem and leadership.

Pros:

- Most of the trouble that young people get into is because they don't believe in themselves or have anyone to show them the right way.
- If students learned to be leaders, they wouldn't follow bad advice and get involved in crime.
- Such classes would force the students to spend more time focusing on positive things so they would have less time to get into trouble.

Cons:

- There is no proof that crime is caused solely by lack of self-esteem or leadership and not just by greed and selfishness.
- The classes wouldn't necessarily give students self-esteem or leadership skills.
- Increasing students' leadership skills might just make them better criminals.

9 People, no matter their religion or culture, have the same core beliefs.

Pros:

- Almost all religions have the same core belief of being kind to other people.
- Many people feel that all religions are essentially the same anyway, just with different names for a central spirit.
- Differences in cultures and religions are mostly because of external things, like climate and topography.

CHAPTER
7

Cons:

- Some societies value violence and others value peace, even when their citizens claim to belong to the same religion.
- Differences in religions are not always in doctrine, but are culturally different, such as the extreme differences between Buddhism and Roman Catholicism.
- Differences in cultures and religions come from the people who form them, so they must have different beliefs.

10 It is better to ask forgiveness after you have done something than permission before you do it.

Pros:

- Red tape prevents things from getting done, even if they are positive.
- Sometimes change is painful, so people are afraid to let it happen.
- People in power in a situation obviously don't want things to change, even if the change would be better for the majority.

Cons:

- Breaking the rules may be effective, but it eats away at society.
- Rules are designed to make things equal for everyone, not just the strongest or most daring people who are willing to break them.
- If a change needs to happen, it will eventually happen anyway.

11 For many students, leaving high school and entering college or the work force will completely change the social rules by which they have been living for the past few years. What, in your opinion, is the best way to navigate a new social situation?

The best way is to observe the social scene for a week or two before acting.

- At first it may look like one group is popular or fun, but you can't know until you see everyone in the group.
- Once you've figured out the hierarchy and decided what group you want to be part of, you should join that group.

12 Some people say that the United States should become more aggressive in mediating disputes in other parts of the world, while others think the United States should focus more on domestic problems. If you could decide what the

United States should do, what would be the three most important decisions you would make and why?

Sample Response 1: I would keep the U.S. focussed more on domestic problems.

- I would recommend health care for everyone, not just people who work at "normal" jobs.
- I'd find a solution to the Social Security problem—either fix it or get rid of it.
- I'd fix education so we can be number one in developing new technologies again.

Sample Response 2: I would keep the U.S. focussed more on foreign policy.

- I would create a Palestinian state to solve the crisis in the Middle East.
- I would take over the governments of the countries in Africa who are involved in civil wars.
- I would take over financial management of the countries in Latin America with economic problems.

13. What are the qualities that make a person a genius? How can we tell the difference between a true genius and a very smart person?

To be a genius, a person must be absolutely dedicated to his or her chosen field.

- Geniuses must also have unnatural gifts or ties to their fields that can't be developed just by practice.
- A true genius is someone who has a sharp focus on one specific thing, while a smart person knows less about more things. Anyone can develop knowledge by practice, but a genius has a connection to the subject that is innate.

14. Assume that you have a job that pays you more than enough to live on and meet your basic needs. What would you do with the excess money you made? Would you save it or spend it and why?

I would save it for retirement.

- I'd rather be able to know I would be able to retire at least as well as I lived.
- I would want to be able to travel when I had free time, and not worry about medical care.
- I would also like to be able to help my children and grandchildren financially.

PT/HSPA, FCAT, MEAP HST, MCAS, GEE21, Regents Exams, SOL, NCCT, AHSGE, GHSGT, E
NCCT, AHSGE, GHSGT, BST, BSAP, WASL, CAHSEE, TAAS, OGT /HSPA, FCAT, MEA
GT, HSPT/HSPA, FCAT, MEAP HST, MCAS, GEE21, Regents Exams OL NCCT, AHSGE, GI

CHAPTER
7

WRITING

15 Do you think that different generations can ever understand one another's experiences? If so, how? If not, why?

Yes: Generations can understand each other's emotions like fear, anger, and love.

- It doesn't matter if they can understand individual experiences.
- They can get beyond nostalgia or focus on the present to put themselves in each other's places emotionally.

No: Differing generations can't relate to the experiences of the other generation's time period.

- Only those who fought in Vietnam understand what it was like to be in the Vietnam War.
- Each generation cannot get beyond feeling that their own generation is the best.
- Differing generations can love each other; they just may not truly understand each other.

16 What are the most important qualities to you in a work situation? What would your ideal job consist of?

Praise, high salary, and a fast pace are the most important qualities.

- I'd enjoy working in a high-pressure situation.
- My ideal job would be in sales or something that had high pressure but also lots of recognition and a huge salary.

17 What do you think are the most important values that parents should teach their children? Why?

Parents should teach their children kindness to others, self-esteem, and generosity.

- Kindness will make them treat others with respect.
- Self-esteem will allow them to love themselves and others.
- Generosity will make them give more to the world than they take.

18 Think about the person that you consider to be your major role model. What qualities does this person have that makes you want to emulate him or her?

My mother is my role model.

- My mother is patient, even with people who are not as smart as she is.
- She is loving and takes care of her family.
- She is concerned with justice and fights to help underdogs in society.

19 How do you define patriotism? Does the definition of patriotism depend on the system of government within a given country? Explain.

Patriotism is pride in one's country.

- In a democracy, patriotism means that you can love the country even if you don't agree with everything it does.
- In a country controlled by one person or idea, patriotism means being loyal and not asking questions.
- In some countries, patriotism means hating anyone from another country or system of government.

20 What do you think are the principal skills you will need to become successful in life?

I will need focus, self-esteem, and empathy for others.

- Focus will allow me to set a goal and work toward it constantly without getting distracted.
- Self-esteem will allow me to love myself and know that I can do whatever I decide to.
- Empathy will help me think of others and avoid hurting people on my path to success.

21 Tell about why you feel proud of your heritage. If you aren't proud of your heritage, explain why.

Taking part in the Annual Puerto Rican Day festival made me proud of my heritage.

- I am proud to be part of such a varied and interesting ethnic group and of the exciting culture I was raised in.
- I am proud to be bilingual and able to understand two cultures—the United States and Puerto Rico.
- I am proud of my family's closeness and our focus on education.

CHAPTER
7

22 If you could see into the future, what are some of the changes you think we will see in the world in the next fifty years?

- We will be able to convert pollution into fuel.
- We will be able to travel more quickly and without as much hassle.
- We will have developed some sort of system for countries to solve their problems without resorting to violence.

23 What do you think a child's responsibility is to his parents, if any?

- It depends on the way the parents treated the child.
- If the parents treated the child well, the child should house, feed, and clothe the parents.
- Many children choose to do more than this out of love.

24 Do you think a politician's primary responsibility is to vote according to his or her own will or the will of the constituents that elected him or her? Why? A politician should vote according his or her own will.

- Constituents elect politicians based on past accomplishments and record, not just as a stand-in.
- If a politician's only job is to vote the will of the constituents, then anyone could be a politician and it wouldn't matter who won an election.
- Most people understand that politicians are pulled in different directions, so they know that a politician will usually vote his or her own will anyway.

25 Do you think there are any occupations for which one gender is more suited than the other? Why or why not?
There is no real difference.

- An obvious exception is the job of mother and father, but those aren't really occupations.
- Most differences just result from tradition and sexism.
- The use of modern technology eliminates most gender differences in jobs.

WRITING

Exercise 2: Sample Paragraphs

The following paragraphs are based upon *one* of the points outlined in Exercise 1.

1. Without art, life is meaningless.

   Brainstorming Point: Art provides relief from the daily grind.

   > The main way in which art gives life meaning is by giving us relief from the daily grind. In modern society so many of us are rushing around constantly trying to get things done that we just don't take time to stop and look at the beauty of life. Also, much of what we encounter just isn't beautiful, like traffic, our schools, office buildings, and the subway or bus. Art provides relief from these ugly things by making us look at something beautiful or just interesting. It makes us slow down to think about the way the artist uses color or symbolizes something or looks at something in a new way. In short, art makes us stop and reexamine life and beauty.

2. A person should choose the career that will pay the most.

   Brainstorming Point: Choosing a low-paying career may contribute more to society by filling valuable occupations like teaching or social work.

   > Finally, it is better to take a lower-paid but valuable career like teacher or social worker than a higher-paid but socially worthless career like stockbroker or corporate lawyer. While there is no doubt that people with higher-paying jobs contribute to the economy by buying more things and paying more taxes, people with more valuable careers contribute a lot more to the world in general. The world could simply not survive without people who were willing to miss out on expensive clothes and vacations to educate children or help poor people. The idea that a career is only important because it pays a lot of money is very materialistic and doesn't show the real value of humanity.

3. No one is an island.

   Brainstorming Point: The greatest joys in life come from forming relationships with others.

   > Another reason it is true that no one should be an island is that the greatest joys in life come from forming relationships with other people. One example is my uncle, who was a loner for years and years. He sup-

PT/HSPA, FCAT, MEAP HST, MCAS, GEE21, Regents Exams, SOL, NCCT, AHSGE, GHSGT,
NCCT, AHSGE, GHSGT, BST, BSAP, WASL, CAHSEE, TAAS, OGT, T/HSPA, FCAT, MEA
GT, HSPT/HSPA, FCAT, MEAP HST, MCAS, GEE21, Regents Exams OL, NCCT, AHSGE, GH
GHSGT, BST, BSAP, WASL, CAHSEE, TAAS, OGT, HSPT/HSPA, FCAT, MEAP HST, MCAS,

CHAPTER
7

ported himself and had people to hang out with, but no one he really thought of as a true friend, and no long-term romantic relationships. Then, he met the lady who is now my aunt and decided to break out of his prison of isolation to give the relationship his all. They got married and had a baby, who is now my 10-year-old cousin Jimmy. My uncle always says that he can't imagine how horrible his life would be now if he didn't have my aunt and Jimmy.

4. You can tell what the ideals of a society are by the way it treats children.

Brainstorming Point: Since children learn to act the way people treat them, it's a never-ending circle.

Another thing to consider is that children respond to the way they are treated. So if they are told repeatedly that they are worthless, they will act as if they are worthless. If a society doesn't treat children well, those same children will grown up not only to treat other children poorly, but also to be violent and hateful. There is no hope for a society like this, since everyone alive will be someone who was treated poorly as a child, so no one will have any idea how to break out of the cycle of abuse and degradation. In contrast, a society that values children tends to have adults who respect themselves and others and also treat children well, thus continuing the circle.

5. All high school students should be required to volunteer a certain number of hours if they want to graduate.

Brainstorming Point: Students will only develop bad attitudes about helping others by being forced to volunteer.

While it's understandable that adults want to instill a spirit of volunteering and helping others in high school students, forcing them to do community service will probably backfire. Instead of becoming filled with the joy of helping others, the high school students will probably resent the fact that they have to spend time doing something they didn't choose to do. After all, teenagers already resent the fact that they aren't in control of their own lives because they have to go to school five days a week. Adding more "volunteer" hours on top of that will just make them even more resentful. So instead of raising new generations of volunteers, forcing students to help others if they want to graduate will actually just create new generations of people who don't want to volunteer.

6 People today are less polite than they were in the past.

Brainstorming Point: Life moves faster, so there's no time for social politeness.

One important reason for the decrease in politeness is the rise of technology and fast pace of modern society. In the past, people had time to stand around and make polite comments to each other since they were already waiting for something to happen, whether it was for a letter to arrive or for someone to cook a homemade meal. Now we have faxes, e-mail, cell phones, and fast food. These things were supposed to make everything more convenient so we would have less to do, but instead, we are expected to do more. That leaves us no time to make polite chit-chat because we have to be getting things done at the speed of light. My mother told me that when she was in college she would pay someone else to type her papers for her on a typewriter and would sit around talking with other people waiting to get their typed papers. This is very different from my older sister's experience, which is writing a paper on her computer and then uploading it to a web page so her professor only has to click the link to read it. My sister doesn't have any down time to sit around talking. Modern life forces us to do more, so we don't have time for old-fashioned manners.

7 Movies and television producers pay more attention to advertisers than they do to the public.

Brainstorming Point: Wholesome family programming is considered to be "uncool," so advertisers don't support it, and it doesn't get made.

The kind of wholesome family programming that doesn't glorify sex and violence is considered by many to be "uncool," so it doesn't get made. The few shows that do fit this category tend to be viewed by older people, and advertisers always want something that appeals to younger people. This is why advertisers think of slogans like "Drink Young" for Pepsi. Some of these shows have been very popular with the public, but advertisers still don't seem to want to be associated with them. They act as if older people don't have any money to spend. This means that ultimately television networks and movie studios don't make as many family programs because they can't sell ads on them, even though people would watch them. Although it seems kind of dumb, it ultimately affects the way we think as a society because we keep seeing all the "young" violent and sexual programming instead of family things we would all be willing to watch.

[8] Society could decrease the level of crime by providing high school students with classes on self-esteem and leadership.

Brainstorming Point: Increasing students' leadership skills might just make them better criminals.

> An unintentional consequence of making students take leadership classes would be training them to be better criminals. They could use the skills they learn in class about how to lead people, organize, and strategize to become even better at selling drugs or stealing cars. It would work the same way it often does when someone goes to jail and instead of being rehabilitated comes out having learned all sorts of new kinds of crimes and ways to avoid being caught the next time. The only real way to ensure that this didn't happen would also be to make sure students had good futures to look forward to once they got out of school, instead of just being set free to roam around and try to support themselves without any support from society. Leadership without moral values is worse than a simple lack of moral values.

[9] People, no matter what religion or culture they belong to, have the same core beliefs.

Brainstorming Point: Many people feel that all religions are essentially the same anyway, just with different names for a central spirit.

> Also, it is the belief of many people that different religions are all just worshiping the same spirit, or guiding force. They feel that no matter what name a religion gives it, whether it's God, Allah, Jehovah, chi, or something else, it's all the same life-giving force. If the thing you worship is all the same, then the core beliefs of the different religions can't be very different. We know that this is true for most of the major religions, like Judaism, Christianity, Islam, and Buddhism. All of these religions believe that life should be respected and that killing is wrong. They also all believe in peace and justice. Of course there are some exceptions, such as Satanism, but the majority of the people in the world have these core beliefs because their religions are essentially worshiping the same thing.

[10] It is better to ask forgiveness after you have done something than permission before you do it.

Brainstorming Point: Red tape prevents things from getting done, even if they are positive.

First, it is often better for everyone to do something first and ask questions later. Modern society has so much red tape and bureaucracy involved in almost anything you want to do that it is often nearly impossible to get anything done. In situations like this, the only ethical thing to do is simply do what needs to be done, and then let the people in charge know about it later. For example, my house is a few houses off the regular bus route to the elementary school my little brother goes to. The bus driver noticed that my brother had to walk to school, even though he only lived two houses closer to the school than did some of the kids who were allowed to ride the bus. So every day she just started stopping in front of our house and letting my brother ride the bus. She did that every day for two years until the principal of the school found out. The principal told her she had to stop, but when the bus driver said she'd been doing it for two years the principal let her keep on doing it. In this situation, my brother would have had to walk to school every day if the bus driver had asked for permission before she did anything.

11 For many students, leaving high school and entering college or the work force will completely change the social rules they have been living with for the past few years. What, in your opinion, is the best way to navigate a new social situation?

Brainstorming Point: At first it may look like one group is popular or fun, but you can't know until you see everyone in the group.

The main reason you should wait a little while before you join a group is because you can't always know what a group is really like until you see most of the people in it. It may turn out that you don't want to be part of that group after all, but once you've become friends with one group, it's hard to just disappear and join another one. I had this exact problem when I went to summer camp for a month the summer after eighth grade. I quickly became friends with two girls in my cabin, but soon I found out that they were in the group of friends led by a girl named Chelsea who thought that she was the most popular girl in the world. Chelsea bossed everyone around and was only interested in clothes and talking about boys. I wanted to play sports and talk about music, but no one else in the group would because they were too busy trying to make Chelsea happy. Eventually, I did find other friends who wanted to do the things I like, but in the meantime I was really unhappy hanging around with Chelsea, and when I left the group they were all really mean about it.

12 Some people say that the United States should become more aggressive in mediating disputes in other parts of the world, while others think the United States should focus more on domestic problems. If you could decide what the United States should do, what would be the three most important decisions you would make and why?

Brainstorming Point: I'd find a solution to the Social Security problem—either fix it or get rid of it.

> Another thing I would do would be to make one final decision about what we should do with our Social Security system. Either we need to get rid of it completely and let everyone in the country be responsible for his or her own retirement savings, or we need to fix it so that it can keep running and paying out money to the people who pay into it. As it is right now, no one seems to know if Social Security will even be around for people my age. But in the meantime, people my age are paying lots of our hard-earned money into the system. I remember how shocked I was when I got my first paycheck at my job last summer. I couldn't believe how much work I'd done just so that my money could go into the Social Security system. I am sure that everyone in the country would rather know that they are going to be taken care of when they retire, or else they get to keep their money now to invest as they want to.

13 What are the qualities that make a person a genius? How can we tell the difference between a true genius and a very smart person?

Brainstorming Point: Geniuses must also have unnatural gifts or ties to their fields that can't be developed just by practice.

> Another thing that makes a person a genius is that the person must have some strange, almost unnatural tie to whatever subject he or she is a genius in. This tie is something that can't be developed just by practice, but must be something that the person was born with. For example, Mozart was a musical genius, and he started composing when he was a very young child. He didn't have the time to study music long enough to be able to compose, but he started doing it anyway because he had a special sense about music. In contrast, there are many, many people who are really good at music, but they can't be considered to be geniuses because their talent is developed through long hours of study and practice, not something that they were born with. Of course, this doesn't mean that geniuses don't have to study and practice; it just means that they also have something more that makes them good at their chosen fields.

14 Assume that you have a job that pays you more than enough to live on and meet your basic needs. What would you do with the excess money you made? Would you save it or spend it and why?

Brainstorming Point: I would also like to be able to help my children and grandchildren financially.

> The final reason I would save my money instead of spending it is because I want to be able to help any children and grandchildren I might have. I think it is really important for families to stick together, and I would never want to feel like I had lived a fancy life when I was young just to leave my family struggling later. I would rather live more calmly, without spending all my money, and then be able to help my children go to college and buy houses and send their own children to college. This would make me much happier than spending money on clothes or cars or trips or other things in the short term.

15 Do you think that different generations can ever understand one another's experiences? If so, how? If not, why?

Brainstorming Point: Generations can understand each other's emotions like fear, anger, and love.

> I would argue that it isn't really important to understand the specific experiences of a generation, since many experiences will never be repeated again. For instance, we will never fight another war the way we fought the Korean War. However, if we can understand the common emotions that all of us feel at one time or another, then it doesn't matter if we can actually picture ourselves in the exact same outfit in the exact same place saying the exact same words. I can read the letters my grandmother wrote to my grandfather when he was serving in the Navy and understand what it was like for her even though I have never been in that situation just because I also know what it feels like to be in love, to be lonely, and to miss someone.

16 What are the most important qualities to you in a work situation? What would your ideal job consist of?

Brainstorming Point: My ideal job would be in sales or something that had high pressure but also lots of recognition and a huge salary.

> Since I know all these things about myself, I think that my ideal job would be in a field like sales. In sales, I would be expected to work really

hard and under a lot of pressure, but where I would also make a huge salary and would get praise from my superiors for a job well done. I can't imagine doing something slow-paced like woodworking, or relaxed, like party planning. Those careers would bore me to tears, even if I could make a lot of money doing them. I have so much energy that I can't just sit around doing nothing, so a career that sucked up a lot of that energy would be perfect for me. I'm also very good with people, so sales would be a natural thing for me to go into.

17 What do you think are the most important values that parents should teach their children? Why?

Brainstorming Point: Self-esteem will allow them to love themselves and others.

Self-esteem is one lasting gift parents can give their children. Without self-esteem, a child cannot love himself enough to make good choices. Most of the kids who go on drugs, join gangs, or commit crimes do so because they don't have self-esteem and can't understand that they deserve a better life. If parents who taught them to love themselves had raised them, they wouldn't be tempted to do things that are bad for them. Once you love yourself, you can begin to love others and treat them the way they should be treated, too. If a person doesn't have self-esteem, he can't love someone in a healthy way. It will either be a desperate love or a false love. So, it's important to teach children self-esteem so they can form normal, healthy relationships with others.

18 Think about the person that you consider to be your major role model. What qualities does this person have that makes you want to emulate him or her?

Brainstorming Point: My mother is patient, even with people who are not as smart as she is.

My mother is an extremely patient person, even with people who are not as smart as she is. She probably learned to be so patient when she was a special education teacher. All the kids in her classes used to have learning or behavioral problems, and lots of them had been told they were stupid by other teachers or by their parents. My mom tried to see the best in every child, even when the child wasn't acting very lovable or smart. She always treated my brothers and me the same way and was gentle and patient with us even when we didn't really deserve it. I am a

WRITING EXERCISES

very impatient person, but I am trying to teach myself to be more patient, like my mother. It seems to bring her so much joy to be calm and helpful instead of cranky and stressed when someone doesn't do something right the first time, and I'd like to feel like she does.

19 How do you define patriotism? Does the definition of patriotism depend on the system of government within a given country? Explain.

Brainstorming Point: In a democracy, patriotism means that you can love the country even if you don't agree with everything it does.

In a democracy, or at least in the United States, part of patriotism is having the right and duty to voice disagreement with something the country does and by doing so show your love for the country. Since our country is founded on the principles that each person has the right to think for him- or herself and to speak his or her own mind, it would be unpatriotic of an American not to speak up when he or she thinks something is going wrong. Of course, because a democracy means that the majority opinion rules, speaking up does not always make you popular. For example, many people hated Martin Luther King, Jr. He saw all the racism in the United States and not only spoke out about it but also organized a civil rights movement. There were lots of people who wanted him dead, and he was ultimately killed by an assassin. But he is considered a great patriot because he loved his country enough to point out the things wrong with it. This is the major difference between patriotism in a democracy and in countries with other forms of government.

20 What do you think are the principal skills you will need to become successful in life?

Brainstorming Point: Focus will allow me to set a goal and work toward it constantly without getting distracted.

The most important skill I will need to have to be successful in life is the ability to focus. Almost all successful people say that what got them to where they are was setting goals and following through until they met those goals. To achieve your goals, you have to have the focus to do all the steps necessary to reach the end of the journey. Without focus, you end up wasting energy on distractions instead of staying on the path you have set for yourself. At times the path to your ultimate goal may seem tedious or uninteresting. However, if you stay focused and push through to the end, you will really have some—

thing to show for it, instead of just a bunch of distractions that were fun at the time but don't amount to anything.

[21] Tell about why you feel proud of your heritage. If you aren't proud of your heritage, explain why.

Brainstorming Point: I am proud of my family's closeness and our focus on education.

One aspect of my heritage that I am especially proud of is my family's closeness and our focus on education. Everyone knows that Puerto Rican families stick together through good times and bad times and support each other no matter what. I think people who are not Puerto Rican don't understand that we aren't just a bunch of happy-go-lucky people who are always dancing and singing and looking for a party. A strong aspect of Puerto Rican culture is the quest for education. Parents are never more proud of their children than when they are studying or earning a degree. For us it is seen not just as a way to gain a better financial situation, but also as a way to expand our minds.

[22] If you could see into the future, what are some of the changes you think we will see in the world in the next fifty years?

Brainstorming Point: We will be able to convert pollution into fuel.

One important change that will happen is that we will develop the technology to convert pollutants into fuel. This will solve two of our current major problems. For one thing, we will no longer have to dirty the air, land, and water by just spewing pollution out into the world. Instead, we'll harness it to convert it into fuel. For another thing, we won't have to continue to use up all our natural resources, like trees, coal, and petroleum, as fuel. Instead, we'll just use our never-ending supply of pollution. Leaving our natural resources intact and not releasing any more pollution into the environment will make things cleaner and will help the earth begin to heal itself after all our years of abusing it.

[23] What do you think a child's responsibility is to his parents, if any?

Brainstorming Point: If the parents treated the child well, the child should house, feed, and clothe the parents.

Before we make up a list of things that a child should do for his or her parents, we first have to know how the parents treated the child. If the parents were loving and supported the child, then the child has more responsibility to help the parents at all stages of life, not only when they are older and less able to care for themselves. Some parents either aren't present while their children grow or treat their children badly. In these cases, I think the child doesn't have any responsibility to take care of or help the parents at all. In some cases, in fact, I think the best thing would be for the child never to have contact with the parents again. For the rest of the argument, however, let's assume that the parents were good parents who did everything they could for the child.

24 Do you think a politician's primary responsibility is to vote according to his or her own will or the will of the constituents that elected him or her? Why?

Brainstorming Point: If a politician's only job is to vote the will of the constituents, then anyone could be a politician and it wouldn't matter who won an election.

There are some people who will argue that since the constituents elect a politician, it is the politician's job to do what the constituents want. The flaw in this argument, however, is that if an elected official only had to vote the way the constituents wanted, then it wouldn't matter who was elected. There would be no difference at all between candidates, no matter what party they represented or what views they had. A politician wouldn't have to have any experience or education whatsoever. But the fact is that there is fierce competition for elected positions, and politicians take great care to make their differences obvious to the voting public. Voters vote for the person whose views most closely match up with their own because they want someone who thinks like they do to represent them in government.

25 Do you think there are any occupations for which one gender is more suited than the other? Why or why not?

Brainstorming Point: Most differences just result from tradition and sexism.

There are many occupations that were traditionally thought to be better suited for one gender or the other. For example, women were thought to be better nurses and teachers, while men were thought to be better police officers, firemen, and soldiers. However, those ideas were only based on tradition and sexism. Many firemen, for instance, thought that women couldn't do the job only because they had never seen a woman do it. They also built themselves up by acting very macho, and

WRITING

this created an attitude that women were inferior to men. Now that women are active firefighters, it is obvious that they can do it as well as men can. The only reason they were barred from this occupation before was because people didn't know any better. This is the case with virtually all of the gender-typed occupations.

Writing Exercises

For each essay topic, assess the topic, brainstorm, organize, write, revise, rewrite, and proofread. There is a scoring guide on page 192 and sample essays for all the topics beginning on page 193.

1. Write an essay in which you examine how art has had an impact on your life or on the life of someone else.

2. In attempting to make a decision, some people try to compromise, while others try to enforce their own opinion. Write an essay in which you examine how this choice affects the people involved in the decision.

3. Write an essay in which you examine how your family dynamics affect the way you approach friendships.

4. Write an essay in which you examine how religious beliefs can affect the way a person makes ethical decisions.

5. Write an essay in which you examine how school can have an impact on a person's self-esteem.

6. Write an essay in which you examine how your ethnic background shapes your thoughts about education.

7. Some people in our country have an easier time obtaining justice than others do. Write an essay in which you examine how this inequality affects society as a whole.

8. In some segments of society, violence is seen as less acceptable than in other segments. Write an essay in which you examine how this difference may have developed.

9. Some people are overly conscious of racial difference, while others feel that it has no importance whatsoever. Write an essay in which you examine how these two points of view can affect an individual's behavior

in social situations.

10 The idea of the undereducated person who works hard to make a better life is a strong part of the American culture. Write an essay in which you examine how this idea affects the work ethic of people of your generation.

11 Write a letter to the head of your local school board arguing that the school day should start and end 45 minutes later.

12 Write a letter to your city council requesting that fines be doubled for parking in disabled parking spaces without a permit.

13 Write a letter to your math teacher, Mr. Pederson, asking to be allowed to miss the final to go to your sister's wedding.

14 Write a letter to the Living Classroom program recommending your favorite teacher to spend a month in a special biosphere.

15 Write a letter to the president expressing your opinion on welfare reform.

16 Write a letter to your community college requesting a course catalogue and information about registering for classes.

17 Write a letter to the editor of your local newspaper arguing in favor of raising the minimum wage.

18 Write a letter to the director of an amusement park requesting an interview for a job for the summer.

19 Write a letter to a camera manufacturer asking for a replacement for the camera that broke the first day you used it.

20 Write a letter to your 10th grade science teacher, Ms. Alexakis, asking for a letter of recommendation for a special science summer program.

21 Which is more important: duty to yourself or duty to others?

22 No one can be completely successful at work and also have a happy family life. Do you agree or disagree with this statement? Why?

23 Is honesty the best policy? Why or why not?

24 Which statement has more value: "Never judge a book by its cover" or "The first impression is the lasting impression"?

25 Have computers improved the quality of life? Why or why not?

Scoring Guide and Sample Essays

Obviously, there's no single correct way to write any of the essays in this book. This means that instead of having an answer key for the essay section, we're giving you a series of questions designed to help you score your own essay. The most useful way to write and score your essays will be to go one at a time, first writing an essay, then evaluating it, and finally, rewriting it based on the weaknesses you uncovered in your evaluation.

If you happen to be studying for the writing exam with a friend, it would be beneficial for the two of you to exchange essays and evaluate each other's work.

> It can be extremely helpful to have another person's opinion on your writing (that's why most book authors belong to writing groups—to get helpful critiques of their work).

Often, someone else can see both strengths and weaknesses in your writing that you can't see on your own.

We're also providing a sample essay for each topic. These essays are meant only as rough guides and examples of how the question could be approached. Your essay can look very different from ours and still be a high-scoring essay. If you're having problems approaching a particular question, however, sometimes it can be helpful to see how someone else wrote on that same topic. So, our essays should be used to help you in the writing process, but not as absolute standards.

Please note that the opinions expressed in the essays, brainstorming notes, or in any other examples in this book do not reflect the views of the publisher, editor, or author of the book. They are just examples to show how a student could answer a question if he or she chose.

Scoring Guide

You'll notice that the following questions were covered in the chapter on writing. Be sure to think them through thoroughly and answer them honestly. If you don't think you can, ask someone else to read your essay and answer the questions about it.

- ✓ Did I answer the question directly?

- ✓ Did I stick to the point throughout the paper, without going off on any tangents?

- ✓ Can you tell from the first paragraph what the point of the paper is?

- ✓ Is my argument easy to follow, or is the paper vague or confusing in parts?

- ✓ Have I made any major grammatical mistakes?

- ✓ Did I use slang or other non-standard English?

- ✓ Did I back up any points I made with evidence or reasoning?

- ✓ Did I avoid redundancy and padding?

- ✓ Did I write a conclusion paragraph that makes a strong finish?

If you did well on those questions, go deeper and answer these questions about the details of the essay.

Did you find . . .

- ✓ Sentences without subjects or verbs?

- ✓ Sentences with mismatched subjects and verbs?

- ✓ Incorrect pronouns?

- ✓ Verb tense errors?

- ✓ Misplaced modifiers (words or phrases)?

- ✓ Mismatched comparisons or lists of things?

- ✓ Sentences that are too long and complicated?

- ✓ Sentences that are too simple?

- ✓ Too many sentences that sound alike?

- ✓ Language that is too casual or simple, or overly difficult?

If you don't think you did a very good job, go back and try again. Keep practicing and assessing your work until you are satisfied that you wrote a good essay.

SAMPLE ESSAYS

[1] Write an essay in which you examine how art has had an impact on your life or on the life of someone else.

I feel strongly that art can have a direct influence on people's lives. It may be as small as brightening someone's day or causing someone to think about a topic they had never explored before. However, sometimes art's effect can be much greater. In the following essay I'll explain one way in which art changed the life of one of my family members.

When my uncle was in the hospital with intestinal problems, he was in extreme pain. My aunt brought him a painting that he had in his office at home because she knew he loved it. It wasn't a famous painting, but his father painted it when he was young, and it really expressed my uncle's father's joyful spirit.

The whole three weeks my uncle was in the hospital, he would spend hours each day just looking at that painting. One of the nurses commented that he had been using a lot more pain medication before my aunt brought the painting. My uncle really felt that having the painting there and looking at it instead of the boring hospital walls brought him relief from pain and helped him heal more quickly than he would have otherwise.

Of course, there's no way to know for sure if the painting did have any effect on his pain tolerance or healing rate. What matters is that he thought it did, so he felt better when the painting was there for him to look at. He's been out of the hospital for two years now, and he still makes sure to look at the painting (which is back on the wall in his home office) at least once a day. He credits that painting with restoring his vitality when he was extremely weak, and maybe even saving his life.

In conclusion, I don't think my uncle's story is at all unusual. Healing from illness because of beautiful art or music or literature is probably an "everyday miracle," and may be at least as common as near-death experiences are. But that doesn't mean that its impact on my uncle's life wasn't significant. Because of that, I believe strongly in the healing power of art.

[2] In attempting to make a decision, some people try to compromise, while others try to enforce their own opinions. Write an essay in which you examine how this choice affects the people involved in the decision.

When a group of people try to make a decision, they need to know whether the decision will be made on the basis of consensus, majority rule, or absolute power. People will usually base their actions around the way in which the decision will be made. For instance, a shy person will probably be more comfortable speaking up in a process in which the group must reach consensus than in one in which one person gets to overrule everyone else. A person who knows that she is good at persuading other people to do what she wants doesn't have any reason to join a group that uses consensus. This means that people who choose the groups they belong to are usually satisfied with the process of decision-making, even if they're not that happy about the actual result.

Sometimes, however, people don't have any idea how a group makes decisions. This is when feelings get hurt and people get angry. This probably happens most often when people try to enforce their own opinions upon others. In the process of trying to argue their own opinions, many times people sink to accusing other people of having "wrong" opinions or even insult them personally. So what should have been a calm, rational discussion becomes an all-out fight. The losers of the process end up feeling hurt, used, and resentful. Even the winner can feel tired and resentful, if not ashamed.

Even though consensus seems to be a better way to make decisions without hurting anyone's feelings, this method of decision-making has problems, too. The group has to discuss the situation over and over again until everyone agrees, so the process can go on for hours or days. And if people really disagree, getting everyone to agree can be extremely difficult. By the time the process is over, everyone in the group can feel exhausted and annoyed with each other. This may make them not want to come together again to make another decision.

On the other hand, sometimes people become much closer after having gone through a difficult decision-making process through consensus. Last year our cheerleading squad had to decide whether we needed new uniforms or not. If we got new uniforms, we thought we would look better at state championships. But getting new uniforms meant doing fundraisers to raise the money to buy them, and some people thought it would be too much work to add to our practice schedule and schoolwork. It took us three whole practices to decide, and a couple of times some people started yelling. But once we decided to get the new uniforms we all felt closer than ever. I hope we don't have to make another decision like that anytime soon, but our team is definitely stronger because we used consensus.

The process you use to make decisions can strongly affect the way people feel about each other and about the decision. There is no one way to decide that guarantees that no one will feel bad, however. The people involved in the process just have to stay as calm as possible and try to see it from the other person's point of view. Then they will be able to come together without fighting.

3 Write an essay in which you examine how your family dynamics affect the way you approach friendships.

I believe the dynamics in my family have affected the way I approach friendships very strongly. I am the middle child of five; I have two older brothers and two younger sisters. My brothers are always rough-housing and horsing around, and many times they include me. They seldom play with my sisters, however, because they are much younger than I am. Because of my relationship with my brothers, I think I look for friends who are very dynamic and athletic, because I look up to my brothers very much. I guess I'm really hoping to find friends who are just like my brothers but are my age.

I also feel a special bond with my little sisters, because we three women have to stick together. As they get older, I want to tell them all about how life works, how to deal with boys, how to use makeup, etc. I take my role as an older sister very seriously, and I have a lot of friends who also have younger siblings and want to be a good example for them.

My relationship with my parents is also very important to me because I have worked hard to earn their trust. My parents are very strict, but I appreciate that they have to be strict because they have five children. Without a strong sense of order in a household of seven different people, life might become very disorganized. Therefore, I am not inclined to be friends with people who just wait around until their parents go out of town so they can have a big party and go crazy. Acting out like that is really just a lame cry for attention, and all it does is show disrespect for the parents that raised you.

Therefore, I conclude that I have found a lot of friends who for the most part think the way that I do regarding the importance of family. I am lucky that I have older brothers to look up to, younger sisters to be a role model for, and parents who trust me to do the right thing. As a result, I feel the dynamics in my family have helped me find friends who feel the same way.

4 Write an essay in which you examine how religious beliefs can affect the way a person makes ethical decisions.

Religious views can both help and hurt a person trying to make ethical decisions. How religious beliefs affect a person's decision-making really depends on the person's understanding of his or her own religion. It also depends on whether you think that it is important for people to develop their own moral codes or just to follow the moral codes of their religions.

If people try to develop their own moral sense apart from just the beliefs of their religions, religious beliefs can hurt them when they are trying to make ethical decisions. For instance, most religions do not have any position on the ethics of recycling. So, people who only look to religion for guidance would not know whether they should recycle or not. They might decide that they need to use what they know about the beliefs of their religion to decide what to do and then decide whether that is something they would personally choose to do. In the recycling example, people might ask themselves what Jesus would do about recycling. Then, based on that guess, they could determine whether that matches what they want to do. If it does, then they know that their own ethical code is the same as the one taught by their religions. If not, then they would have to question whether or not they really believe everything their religion tells them.

If people don't really understand their religions, however, this could make a mess of things. They wouldn't have any idea what their religion thinks of certain situations, so they couldn't judge their own actions at all. This could lead to confusion and stress and might possibly make the person abandon that religion.

If people end up being in conflict with their religious views too often, this can cause a crisis of faith. Either they will look for a different religion, or decide that their own decision-making skills are bad. This is a case in which religion hurts people's ability to make their own ethical decisions. On the other hand, if people are comfortable with the decisions based on their religion, then the religion only helps them make decisions.

In conclusion, the better people understand both themselves and their chosen religions, the more religion will help them make ethical decisions. People who don't know themselves or their religion will always have more trouble making decisions than will those who know who they are and what they stand for. Therefore, we should all try to get to understand ourselves better so that we can make better decisions and help the world to become a more ethical place.

5 Write an essay in which you examine how school can have an impact on a person's self-esteem.

Self-esteem is the most important thing a person can have because the only person you have to deal with at the end of the day is you. A lot of our culture tells us how we should feel about ourselves, as we're somehow supposed to measure up to the thin and good-looking people on TV and in magazines. But I think high school has the greatest impact of all on how we build our self-image, especially because high school students are 1) so young and impressionable, and 2) so obsessed with judging each other.

Fitting into the mainstream is an important part of high school life. There are those who are accepted without much effort, and there are others who bend over backward to make the grade by wearing all the right clothes, saying all the right things, and thinking all the right thoughts, favoring conformity over being an individual. Working so hard to be like everybody else can have serious consequences on how a person develops social relationships, and it can severely hurt one's self-esteem. After all, you can't have esteem for yourself if you don't know who you really are.

Moreover, a person who is not accepted by the popular crowd despite such strenuous efforts might assume that it's because of some flaw in his or her own character. As a result, that person might become overly shy when it comes to meeting new people. The reverse is true as well; a person who makes it with the "in crowd" might develop a degree of arrogance that could also have a permanent impact on his or her personality.

The worst possibility, of course, is that someone might abandon common sense in an attempt to be accepted. I have been told many times about the student at my high school many years ago who, on a dare, drove drunk after a party and wrapped the car around a tree and fractured his leg. If he had a stronger sense of self-esteem, he might have realized how dangerous and irresponsible driving drunk is and said "No."

In conclusion, it takes a strong person to keep a sense of self throughout four years of high school. It's too easy to compromise one's principles in order to fit in, but the most important thing a high school student can do is to remain true to him- or herself, regardless of the consequences. Of course, that is easier said than done.

6 Write an essay in which you examine how your ethnic background shapes your thoughts about education.

I come from a family of Scandinavian descent. My great-grandparents on one side moved here from Norway in the early 1900s and my great-great grandparents on the other side moved here from Denmark in the late 1800s. They all came to become farmers in America where land was plentiful for farming. However, the literacy rate in Scandinavia was very high, even back then, so they were fairly well-educated people.

Even though the next generation grew up in very rural areas, they went to school until they were needed full-time to work on the farm.

My Norwegian great-grandparents had 9 children, though, so not all of them were needed to continue with farm life. My grandfather got to go to the nearest big town to finish his last year of high school and go to college. He worked his way through college by being a night janitor. He graduated as a teacher, and over the course of the next 15 years earned his Ph.D. and became a college professor.

My grandfather met my grandmother at college. She was also the first in her family to be educated past high school, but her family had scrimped and saved, and she won a scholarship. They got married as my father was beginning his Ph.D., and she helped him write his dissertation. They sometimes called it "our Ph.D.," because they both worked so hard on it.

Because my grandparents were both college-educated, it never occurred to them that their children would not be. And, in the same way, my mother met my father at college (as did my aunt and uncle, and another aunt and uncle). They all expected their children to go to college. Now, all my living relatives are college graduates (except for the ones that are not old enough yet).

The real attitude about education in my family is not that it is a way into a better life, but that it is something you are expected to do to expand your mind. We all see it as the only logical next step after high school. I know I will go on to college, and I will expect my children and grandchildren to, also. It seems to be the best way to become a well-rounded person.

7. Some people in our country have an easier time obtaining justice than others do. Write an essay in which you examine how this inequality affects society as a whole.

Most of us seek justice in life because we like to think that those who do right will be rewarded and those who do wrong will be punished. But the idea that some people (mostly the richer ones) have a better chance of obtaining justice (or worse, avoiding it if they have committed a crime) can have a negative impact on society, as those who are unable to obtain justice become frustrated and become prone to act out.

Our country was founded on the idea that "all people are created equal." That might be true, but once people grow up, a great deal of inequality emerges. When it comes to obtaining justice (which usually involves some sort of court battle), the odds heavily favor the person who either knows more about the law (or can hire someone who knows more about the law).

PT/HSPA, FCAT, MEAP HST, MCAS, GEE21, Regents Exams, SOL, NCCT, AHSGE, GHSGT
, NCCT, AHSGE, GHSGT, BST, BSAP, WASL, CAHSEE, TAAS, OGT, HSPA, FCAT, ME
OGT, HSPT/HSPA, FCAT, MEAP HST, MCAS, GEE21, Regents Exams, OL, NCCT, AHSGE, G
E, GHSGT, BST, BSAP, WASL, CAHSEE, TAAS, OGT, HSPT/HSPA, FCAT, MEAP HST, MCA

CHAPTER
7

As usual, the outcome usually favors the one with more money. It requires money to hire a good lawyer, or even to become a good lawyer. And unfortunately, most people with money will use their wealth to avoid justice by finding a good lawyer to defend them in court. Just look at all of the wealthy chief executives of big companies who have re-signed in disgrace but have millions to spend to keep themselves out of jail (and millions more to spend once they are through with the court proceedings).

The illusion of equality is shattered every once in a while on a large scale, and those who feel wronged might feel compelled to burn off their frustration. An example is the Rodney King trial a few years ago, in which four white officers were found not guilty of excessively beating an African-American man, even though the entire episode was caught on video tape. The resultant riots cost Los Angeles millions in rebuilding.

In conclusion, I think the whole idea of this question is very ironic. If some people can get justice (or avoid it) easier than others, then there isn't a lot of true justice in the world. But since all humans are born with the sense that they're just as good as anyone else, the "have-nots" are bound to strike back against the "haves" to get what they believe is rightly theirs.

8. In some segments of society, violence is seen as less acceptable than in other segments. Write an essay in which you examine how this difference may have developed.

Violence is much more acceptable in some segments of society than in other segments. There are several theories about why this happened. I feel that it is because different classes have had different experiences in America, and this explains the difference. I will explain my views fully in the following paper.

In general, the lower economic classes in this country are more accepting of violence as a way to solve problems. This probably happened because the ancestors of the people in the lower classes had extremely rough lives when they first came to the United States. Instead of coming here and immediately becoming storekeepers or doctors, most of them came and were day laborers, sharecroppers, subsistence farmers, or slaves. Their day-to-day lives were filled with brutal, back-breaking work and physical and emotional violence inflicted upon them.

After several generations of this, the people were just so used to this violent and difficult way of life that they began to act violent themselves. Children grew up thinking that violence, insults, and misery were normal and expected. When they had children they treated them the same way, so the cycle continued. Today, the descendants of these unfortunate people have become desensitized to violence and don't think anything of using violence to solve problems.

This is why the people in the most bleak situations, like those in the inner city or in economically depressed areas, are more prone to use violence than are the people who live in more affluent areas. The other simple fact is that it makes more sense to be violent when you are stressed out than when you are not. And the kind of stress a rich person experiences because he needs to land the big account isn't at all similar to the kind of stress a poor person experiences when he or she doesn't know if his or her family will be evicted for not paying the rent. In conclusion, the reason violence is more acceptable in some segments of society than in others is because people in those segments didn't grow up knowing any other way to do things. The only way to stop this violence would be to either help them get out of poverty and stress, or teach them other ways to cope with their depression and anger. This probably won't ever happen, so there will still be violence in America.

9 Some people are overly conscious of racial difference, while others feel that it has no importance whatsoever. Write an essay in which you examine how these two points of view can affect an individual's behavior in social situations.

In general, I feel that most people today think that it is better not to be too aware of racial differences. However, this can lead to some problems in social situations, so some people think that racial differences should be openly acknowledged. In the following paper I will examine the advantages and disadvantages of both ways of dealing with racial differences.

If people do not acknowledge racial differences, this can lead to all sorts of problems and hurt feelings in social situations. People who are not the racial majority in a situation can feel that they are not seen as important or that others make assumptions about them that aren't true. For example, sometimes Asian Americans are seen as being the "model minority" and are lumped in with white people for things like test scores and college admissions. This doesn't acknowledge that the reality of being Asian in this country is different from the reality of being Caucasian. The subcultures are very different. I personally know several Asian-American people who feel that they aren't seen as being important in our society because they are lumped in with white people all the time.

However, if people are overly conscious of racial differences, this can be just as hurtful as not acknowledging them at all. An example of this would be when people send cards and have official performances or programs at the end of the calendar year. Sometimes people make references to Christmas and Hanukkah, but also make a big deal out of wishing any African Americans a Happy Kwanzaa. This singles them out as being different. Instead of just lumping Kwanzaa in with Christmas and Hanukkah, it becomes this big dividing line between African Americans and everyone else. It singles them out as being strange and intrinsically different from the majority. The irony is that most African Americans I know celebrate Christmas, too, even if they don't celebrate Kwanzaa.

The conclusion we should all draw from this is that it's bad to try to gloss over things by ignoring them. People in this country are racially diverse. That's one of the really great things about the United States of America. But it's also bad to make such a big deal out of racial difference that you make people feel uncomfortable. We should just treat people like people, all with individual differences, but all with equal importance.

10 The myth of the uneducated person who works hard to make a better life is a strong part of American culture. Write an essay in which you examine how this idea affects the work ethic of people of your generation.

We have all heard the phrases "only in America" and "the American dream," both of which have come to symbolize what people can achieve in their lifetimes. People can build businesses out of nothing (like Bill Gates and Microsoft) or go from a prisoner in Vietnam to the Senate (like Senator John McCain of Arizona). I think these phrases have become less important to my generation, however, because most of us take the idea that anything is possible for granted.

Older people, like my father, who came here from Armenia in the 1960s, have a much stronger idea of what life in other, more oppressive regimes is like, and they have taken it upon themselves to make the most of the opportunity they have been given to live here. Those of us who were born here and know nothing else are more likely to assume that success is our birthright.

My father flunked his first year of school in the United States because he didn't speak any English. When he finally taught himself English, he passed all his classes with As. He continued this determination and built a dry-cleaning business, and then a chain of dry-cleaning businesses. He is thankful every day for the chance he got to come to America.

My sisters and I, on the other hand, have never known what it was like not to speak English or to be poor. As a result, I think we just don't work as hard as my father does. Once, for example, we were painting the garage. My father finished two walls before I even did half of mine, even though I am younger and taller than he is. He's just more used to working quickly to get things done.

In addition, it has never occurred to us that we wouldn't go to college. As a result, we haven't made any effort to do any work with our hands, but instead do our work on the computer or using our minds. Sometimes my father calls us his "softies" and laughs because he knows we wouldn't have any idea what to do if we had to do manual labor to support ourselves.

To conclude, I think that the American dream myth is almost nonexistent for people my age. I think instead there's a myth that we'll all have an easier life than our parents did. For some of us it will probably be true, but others of us will have a rude awakening when things aren't so easy.

11 Write a letter to the head of your local school board arguing that the school day should start and end 45 minutes later.

Dear Sir:

I am writing to ask you to consider altering the state-mandated school-day schedule by making the school day start and end 45 minutes later. I think students would benefit from the extra sleep in the morning, and I believe the time shift would allow students to devote more time to learning and studying in the middle of the day, when they are at their best.

Teenaged people need a lot more rest than most of us get on a nightly basis. Studies show that the average person aged 13-18 needs nine to ten hours of sleep per night in order to maintain the best health. Unfortunately, most high school students are so consumed by studies and extracurricular activities (not to mention the stress of measuring up to the standards set by our parents), we average only four to six hours of sleep per night.

Starting school at 9:00 rather than 8:15 would give the average student the chance to rest after busy days of school, homework, and whatever other activities we are involved in, and arrive ready to learn and feeling more refreshed. I know I am not a morning person, and a number of my friends are not as well, because we stay up late into the night studying. We would all benefit from an extra hour of sleep.

PT/HSPA, FCAT, MEAP HST, MCAS, GEE21, Regents Exams, SOL, NCCT, AHSGE, GHSGT
NCCT, AHSGE, GHSGT, BST, BSAP, WASL, CAHSEE, TAAS, OGT, /HSPA, FCAT, MEA
GT, HSPT/HSPA, FCAT, MEAP HST, MCAS, GEE21, Regents Exams, SOL, NCCT, AHSGE, G

CHAPTER
7

As far as the end of the school day is concerned, keeping kids a little longer in the afternoon can also be beneficial. With less emphasis on the early morning, students can concentrate better. There are also smaller children who have single or working parents and need to be kept active (but supervised) until their parents can come and collect them.

In conclusion, I sincerely feel that it is in the best interest of students to start and end the school day later than the current schedule dictates. It would help students concentrate better, it would keep kids occupied longer into the afternoon, and it would have no effect on the length of the school day, which is harder to change.

I hope that you will consider my opinion and make this important change that could help so many teenaged people.

Sincerely,

Jin Yoo

12 Write a letter to your city council requesting that fines be doubled for parking in disabled parking spaces without a permit.

To the Llanview City Council:

I am writing this letter to request that you raise the fine for parking in a disabled parking space without a disabled parking sticker from $180 to $360. I realize that to double the fine may seem outrageous to some members of our community, but it is practically nothing when you consider how serious the crime is. Please allow me to explain why I think this crime is so horrible.

Disabled people really need these parking spaces close to stores and offices. Most people immediately think of a person in a wheelchair when they think of a disabled person and wonder what the big deal is to just roll a chair a few more yards. But the reality is that many people with disabilities don't use wheelchairs but may have trouble walking. They may have problems with their legs, breathing problems, tremors, or any number of other disabilities. If they can't be guaranteed a parking space very close to a building, they will not be able to make it from their cars to the building.

If they do not make it from their cars to the building, this means they will have to stay home. If they stay home, they will not be able to get the things they need to survive, like food and clothing, not to mention the things that make life nicer, like books or videos or art supplies. If they want these things, they will have to figure out a way to get them delivered, which usually costs extra. This is a big problem, since most disabled people already live on fixed incomes or incomes that are less than the ones that the general population has. So, in essence, by not having disabled parking spaces, we are reducing the incomes of disabled people even more.

This means that whenever someone who is not disabled parks in a disabled parking space, the able-bodied person is stealing directly from disabled people and restricting their lives. I'm sure that you would be furious if someone didn't let you go to the store. That's how disabled people must feel whenever they try to park and find someone in their space who shouldn't be there.

In conclusion, I feel that because parking in a disabled parking space without a disabled sticker is a crime that directly hurts people, the fine should be much greater than $180 and should be raised to $360. Maybe this would make law-breakers think twice about parking in places they shouldn't. By walking a few extra yards they could save themselves a lot of money and make life easier for someone who needs it. Please consider my proposal and raise the fee.

Sincerely,

Travis Stone

13 Write a letter to your math teacher, Mr. Pederson, asking to be allowed to miss the final to go to your sister's wedding.

Dear Mr. Pederson,

I am writing this letter asking to be allowed to miss my math final on June 5. My older sister is getting married that day in Bridgeport, Connecticut, and I cannot miss the wedding.

My sister asked me to be the maid of honor at her wedding. She and I have been best friends since I was born when she was 6. She has helped me through all of my problems in junior high and high school, and I want to be there for her on her special day.

I can take the final on June 2nd or 3rd, if that is convenient for you. Or, I can write a long paper or do a project instead of taking the exam, and I can turn it in to you on June 3rd. I am not trying to avoid any work. I really want to do my best in this class, even though I have to be in Connecticut on the day of the final.

I can stay after school tomorrow to talk to you about this, if that is convenient for you. Please let me know tomorrow in class.

Thank you,

Maria Ramirez

14   Write a letter to the Living Classroom program recommending your favorite teacher to spend a month in a special biosphere.

> To Whom It May Concern:
>
> I am writing to recommend that you choose my ninth grade science teacher, Ms. Jane Borovsky, to be part of the Living Classroom biosphere project. Ms. Borovsky has all the qualities you are looking for in a teacher and would be an asset to the program. She is an excellent scientist, a caring teacher, and has a wonderful personality.
>
> First, Ms. Borovsky is the best scientist I have ever met. She is always asking questions and wondering how things work. She also just seems to have a brain for science. When we were doing an experiment which involved distilling different substances from a combination of liquids, Ms. Borovsky was always able to guess what they were before we did all the tests to prove it. When we asked her how she did it, she just said, "I had a feeling." Someone with such a great scientific mind will surely be an asset in the biosphere.
>
> Second, she is also the best teacher I have had in high school. She pushes us to do our best at all times, and she really tries to get us involved in the material. In addition, she encourages us to use our everyday lives as miniature science projects. For instance, when my friend Brittany came in with poison ivy on her arm, Ms. Borovsky made us look up cures for poison ivy on the internet. Then we applied three different cures in different spots on Brittany's arm, to see which one worked best. This inspiration will help everyone in the biosphere.
>
> Finally, Ms. Borovsky has a wonderful personality. She is always smiling and laughs whenever anyone makes a funny remark. She isn't afraid to talk to us about real life and doesn't avoid us or act too cool to talk to us if she happens to run into us outside of school. She would definitely get along really well with everyone else in the biosphere and would help bring up everyone's spirits if they got sad or bored.
>
> In conclusion, you should definitely pick Ms. Borovsky to be part of the Living Classroom project. I hope that you will take my recommendation seriously and pick her. You will not be disappointed.
>
> > Sincerely,
> > Erika Parsons

15   Write a letter to the president expressing your opinion on welfare reform.

> Dear Mr. President,
>
> I am writing this letter to express my opinions on how welfare should be reformed. I am in the tenth grade and have been volunteering at a homeless shelter for the last year, so I have seen people who used to

WRITING EXERCISES

be on welfare and are now homeless. I have some ideas about how welfare could be changed to be more fair and more helpful.

To begin, it is not fair to tell people who have been on welfare for years that they have to get off it in thirty days. That is what happened last year in my state, and it didn't work. The politicians said that it would get people into the workforce, but all it seemed to do was get people into the homeless shelters. A person who hasn't had a job in several years is not going to be able to get one in a month that will pay enough to buy food and pay rent.

Also, the real problem for the parents I saw was that the only jobs they could find had long hours, and they didn't have anyone to take care of their children. Welfare could be improved by giving people free or low-cost child care, even if it didn't give them any other money. That way, people could go to work and know that their kids were safe and were learning, instead of roaming the streets or locked in at home so no one could hurt them.

Finally, many of the people I saw were very worried about the fact that they didn't have any health insurance for them or for their children. If something happened and they got sick they had no way to be healed except to go to an emergency room and hope that they would be treated for free. Welfare should allow people to keep their health insurance until they get new insurance from an employer so that they don't have to worry that something will happen and they won't get any help.

In conclusion, I think the main ways in which the welfare system should be reformed are to give people more time to transition from welfare to work, to give people child-care vouchers, and to let them keep their health insurance. This would allow them to support themselves instead of falling through the cracks into homeless shelters. In the end, the whole country would benefit from this because they would be paying more taxes into the system.

Sincerely,

Ismael Habbib

16 Write a letter to your community college requesting to enter the journalism program as a sophomore instead of a freshman.

To Whom It May Concern:

I am writing to request that you allow me to enter the journalism program at Monroe County Community College (MCCC) as a sophomore, not a freshman. I have excellent test scores, four years of journalism experience, and extra credits that should be applied to my record.

I have excellent test scores, which are above the average for the journalism program at MCCC. I scored a 580 on the verbal part of the SAT, which is above the MCCC average of 490 and the journalism program's average of 550. This reflects my strong vocabulary and command of the English language. I have never gotten any grade lower than an A- in any of my English classes. I also scored well on the ACT.

I have been writing for my high school paper for the past four years. I also write articles on my high school's sports teams for our neighborhood weekly newspaper. The other reporters for this paper are adults with college degrees, so I am doing the job of a professional journalist.

I also have six extra college-level credits. I earned these the last two summers by going to a special journalism camp at Denison University. I am enclosing a copy of the transcripts from this program. You will see that I got As in all the courses I took there.

Please allow me to enter the MCCC journalism program this fall as a sophomore. I am qualified to skip a year and will work hard to make sure I pass my classes with flying colors.

Sincerely,

Katie Watson

17 Write a letter to the editor of your local newspaper arguing in favor of raising the minimum wage.

Dear Sir:

I am writing this letter in response to the letter in last Sunday's Letters to the Editor in which a reader stated that the minimum wage should not be raised because this would hurt free enterprise. I strongly disagree with this statement and would like to explain why.

The current minimum wage is extremely low. A single person could barely live on it, let alone a family of two or more. The only way a person here in Milwaukee could survive on minimum wage would be working 60 hours a week every week. This means that when other people are at home with their families or in their beds, a minimum wage earner is still working. This is not fair.

Raising the minimum wage would allow people to work shorter hours and still be able to rent an apartment and pay for food and clothes. This is a basic right of all humans, and we have a duty to make it possible for people to feed their families without going on government assistance.

The reader from last Sunday's paper stated that raising the minimum wage would hurt businesses, but it would actually help businesses in the long run. If the minimum wage were raised, workers would have more money to spend. They would spend this money, and it would go back to the companies. Thus, the companies would make more profits in the long run.

In short, we need to raise the minimum wage because we need to start treating people fairly. The fact that doing this would also help businesses is a nice bonus.

Sincerely,

Terell Johnston

18 Write a letter to the director of an amusement park requesting an interview for a job for the summer.

Dear Employment Director,

I am writing to request an interview for a job working at Great Adventure this summer. I have been going to Great Adventure since I was 10, and I love it. Nothing would make me happier than to work at the park this summer.

I have experience in food service from working at my dad's pizza store. I have been cleaning there for the past four years and working the counter for the past year. My skills are speed, accuracy with the orders, and making change in my head.

I would also love to work on one of the roller coasters. My favorite is the Twisting Dragon because it is the highest, scariest coaster in the park. I have always wanted to be one of the people who makes sure that everyone is belted in safely before the ride starts. I've even been practicing giving the thumbs-up sign.

While food service and roller coasters are my two main areas of interest, I would love to do any job at Great Adventure. I hope that you will contact me about an interview soon. You may call me at home at 609-555-1111. Thank you for your time.

Sincerely,

Joshua Banks

19 Write a letter to a camera manufacturer asking for a replacement for the camera that broke the first day you used it.

To Whom It May Concern:

I am writing to you to ask for a replacement camera for your model XV-500. I bought this camera on March 3, and it broke when I used it for the first time on March 4. I read the instruction book thoroughly before I even put the battery in the camera to make sure I could operate it properly. However, when I pressed the button to pull back the lens cap, the lens cap broke. I took the camera back to the store that I bought it from, but they told me to contact you directly to get a replacement.

My mother bought the same camera as a gift for my grandmother last

Christmas, and she has been very happy with it. So I was very surprised when mine broke before I could even take one picture with it. I hope that you will send me a new camera soon so that I can begin taking pictures.

Sincerely,

Marc Garcia

20 Write a letter to your tenth grade science teacher, Ms. Alexakis, asking for a letter of recommendation for a special science summer program.

Dear Ms. Alexakis,

I am writing to ask you to write a letter of recommendation for me to attend the Montclair University Summer Science Lab program. The program is six weeks in the summer studying biology and chemistry. I am asking you because you taught me biology and can tell them about my love for science.

To refresh your memory, I came to class on time every day. I also stayed after school on Tuesdays to help you set up the dissection projects for your first-period class on Wednesdays. I really love dissecting, since it's the best way to see what's really happening inside an animal.

I also did the two extra credit projects you let us do. The first one was the PowerPoint presentation on photosynthesis, and the second one was the model of the cow's digestive system. You gave me As on both of them, so I ended up with an A+ in your class both semesters.

I really want to go to this program this summer, but it is very competitive. I know that with my grades and a great recommendation letter from you, I can get in.

Thank you so much for your help.

Sincerely,

Chantelle Brown

21 Which is more important: duty to yourself or duty to others?

It is extremely difficult to answer the question of whether duty to yourself or duty to others is more important.

On one hand, duty to yourself could be seen as being the most important thing of all. After all, if you don't look out for yourself, you can't expect anyone else to either. And once you fulfill your duty to yourself, you are free to help others without worrying that you are shortchanging yourself by putting others first. An example of this would be on an airplane. If the pressure changes and the oxygen masks drop down, you are supposed to put your own on first before you help anyone else. This is a metaphor for the rest of life, in that you can't help others if you haven't taken care of your own needs first.

GEE 21, Regents Exams, SOL, NCCT, AHSGE, GHSGT, BST, BSAP, WASL, CAHSEE, TAAS,
WASL, CAHSEE, TAAS, OGT, HSPT/HSPA, FCAT, MEAP HST, MCAS, GEE 21, Regents Exa
Exams, SOL, NCCT, AHSGE, GHSGT, BST, BSAP, WASL, CAHSEE,
FCAT, MEAP HST, MCAS, GEE 21, Regents Exams, SOL, NC

WRITING EXERCISES

On the other hand, duty to yourself could be seen as a selfish choice when others are in need of help. After all, if everyone neglected the needs of other people in favor of their own, there would be little human communication in the world, and the problems that we have would grow bigger and bigger. However, if everyone fulfilled their duty to help others, we would all get exactly what we need from other people. There would be no need to focus on ourselves, since everyone else would be helping us and we would be helping them.

Realistically, however, there's no way everyone would do their duty to others. There will always be selfish people who only look out for themselves. This is especially horrible when they act selfishly but don't even do things that are for their own good. For example, some people think that they have the right to smoke wherever they want to. This is not doing their duty to others because it exposes others to secondhand smoke and also annoys them. But it also isn't duty to self, since smoking will eventually kill you in a gruesome and painful way.

In conclusion, it would be nice if everyone would dedicate themselves to helping other people. But this will never happen, so the best we can hope for is that people truly take themselves seriously and do what is right for themselves. Maybe then they will have some energy left over to help others, even if it isn't their first priority.

22 | No one can be completely successful at work and also have a happy family life. Do you agree or disagree with this statement? Why?

Some people feel that to have a happy family life you have to sacrifice success at work and vice versa. I think this is a simplistic view of success, and that, in fact, you can have both. In the following essay I will show that success at work and at home are not mutually exclusive but are actually related to each other.

The view that success at work prevents a happy family life seems to come from the 1980s, when success was defined as having a high-paying, high-pressure job working demanding hours for inhumane bosses. At the same time, a happy family life meant that the wife had to be at home (or feel guilty if she wasn't) decorating the house, fixing the kids' problems, and being Martha Stewart. There just weren't enough hours in the week to be successful at such a demanding job, and no one could live up to the ideal that a happy family life required perfection.

Things are really different now. Most people don't want to work at jobs that suck up all their time and never let them take the day off to go to a Little League game. People have cell phones and flexible hours, and ask for more vacation time instead of more money when they get hired. Men as well as women take time off from work when their children are born. In addition, so many of the higher-paying jobs available now don't require people to sacrifice their personal lives to get promoted in the company that people don't have to choose between the fast-track job and the slow, lowly job anymore.

At the same time, people have become more relaxed about what a happy family means. It isn't a requirement to have Mom at home full-time making everything look perfect. Instead, parents take turns staying home part or full-time. Lots of mothers and fathers telecommute or have home businesses so they can spend more time with their children. Yet those same people probably consider their work lives to be very successful because they get to control when and where they work.

To sum up, the definition of success at the office has changed so much that it no longer means making extreme personal sacrifices. Instead, it means having more control over your own time and work. At the same time, the rigid roles that used to make a happy family seem like a dream have been relaxed, so as long as everyone in the family is happy with the arrangement, families can make up their own rules. In short, people today don't let society tell them what to do anymore, so they can achieve success at work and at home.

23 Is honesty the best policy? Why or why not?

"Honesty is the best policy" is one of the first sayings we are taught as children because parents want their children to grow up as decent people who tell the truth instead of habitual liars. That is fine for children, but as we mature, we find that being completely honest at all times has its drawbacks. As far as this well-worn cliché is concerned, the best thing to be honest about is the fact that honesty is the best policy most of the time, but there may be a place for falsehoods in certain situations.

Children are told to tell the truth, and that's fine for kids, since parents are usually truthful to their kids (except for things like Santa Claus and the Tooth Fairy). At some point, though, children grow up and realize that some people (not all of them) don't tell the truth. The fact is, however, people who always tell the truth think that everyone else always tells the truth as well (an admirable trait), and this misperception can put you at a disadvantage.

An example would be someone who was looking to buy a used car. If you truthfully say that you really want the car, a dishonest sales person might raise the price on you; more importantly, he or she might also lie about whether the car has ever been in an accident.

There are also those situations when the truth can hurt somebody's feelings. For example, my best friend recently asked me how I liked his new haircut. I thought it was really ugly, but I knew that, if I were totally honest, he would get really depressed and hate his hair until it grew out. Therefore, I told a little lie and said it was nice.

In a perfect world, it would be a great thing if everyone was truly honest with one another and we didn't have to deal with lies and deceit. But we know we don't live in a perfect world. I, for one, intend to try to be honest whenever possible, especially when it comes to people I care about.

24 Which statement has more value: "Never judge a book by its cover" or "The first impression is the lasting impression"?

This is an interesting question, because it reminds me of another two proverbs that contradict each other: "He who hesitates is lost" and "Look before you leap." Both have merit, but they can't both be correct. In the case of this topic, however, I believe the first statement has more value than the second, because one is a response to the other; people are usually very judgmental, and they should be reminded not to be.

It is true that "a first impression is a lasting impression." When I moved to my new school three years ago, I was very hopeful that the students would like me, but I had no idea how to act. I did my best to act cool, but on my third day, I tripped in the lunchroom and dropped by lunch tray, spilling soup all over the floor. To this day, even though I have known my friends for years now, they still call me "Soupy."

I realize I am fortunate that I can look back on the incident and laugh. The other students could have easily dismissed me as some sort of geek, and I could have been ostracized. But the people who became my friends saw beyond the first impression I made and got to know me as a person. Still, that first impression has stayed with me, and I bet these guys will call me "Soupy" until I'm 90 years old.

So, in conclusion, both of these sayings are very commonly heard in modern society, and though they seem to say opposite things, they are actually related. A first impression does make a lasting impression, but that isn't the way it should be. So, if you ever find yourself in the position to judge someone based on a first impression that might not be indicative of that person as a whole, you should remember not to judge a book by its cover.

CHAPTER 7

[25] Have computers improved the quality of life? Why or why not?

Much has been said about how computers make our lives easier. With the click of a mouse, we can pay bills, shop, chat with others, or find the latest news or sports scores. It's true that computers have made finding information a lot easier, but the price of this convenience is a lot higher than people think.

Firstly, I believe computers are removing the human element for our society. Chat rooms are replacing discussions, ATMs are taking over for bank tellers, and online shopping is replacing visits to the store. All of this might appear more convenient, but the downside is that we're becoming lazier and less accustomed to face-to-face contact. If the current pattern continues, there might not be any reason to leave the house in fifty years.

Secondly, computers have made it easier for corporations to spy on us and get an idea of our interests so that they can send us piles of spam e-mails. Some sites, for example, have software that keeps track of our previous purchases and offers recommendations to buy more items that we don't want or need. This type of invasion of privacy makes me think of George Orwell's novel, 1984.

Thirdly, since just about everything is now run by a computer, it is scary to think about what could happen if they break down. I remember how concerned everyone was about the Y2K bug a few years ago, and how it could affect power plants, medical equipment, air traffic control devices, and all sorts of other things that need to function properly all the time. Computers have become so common, we don't even realize what kind of chaos could happen as the result of vandalism or a major malfunction.

I think I am in the minority on this topic, because most people really like computers. But, in my opinion, computers have made us more content to avoid human contact, more susceptible to corporate greed, and more vulnerable to a complete shutdown of important services. Since computers are here to stay, however, it's important for people like me to learn to live with it.

That's it! You're done. Good luck!

WRITING

Notes